Verse by Verse Commentary on the Book of

HEBREWS

Enduring Word Commentary Series
By David Guzik

The grass withers, the flower fades,
but the word of our God stands forever.
Isaiah 40:8

Commentary on Hebrews

Copyright ©2019 by David Guzik

Printed in the United States of America
or in the United Kingdom

Print Edition ISBN: 1-56599-037-4

Enduring Word

5662 Calle Real #184

Goleta, CA 93117

Electronic Mail: ewm@enduringword.com

Internet Home Page: www.enduringword.com

Scripture references, unless noted, are from the New King James Version of the Bible, copyright ©1979, 1980, 1982, Thomas Nelson, Inc., Publisher.

Contents

For Gayle Erwin
A Most Encouraging
Follower of Jesus

Hebrews 1 - A Superior Savior

A. Jesus, the superior Savior.

1. (1-2a) Jesus brought a revelation superior to the prophets of old.

God, who at various times and in various ways spoke in time past to the fathers by the prophets, has in these last days spoken to us by *His* Son,

a. **God**: The Book of Hebrews begins with no mention of the author, only of **God**. The human author of Hebrews remains unknown, but the book's inspiration by the Holy Spirit is evident.

i. The earliest statement on the authorship of Hebrews is from Clement of Alexandria, who said that Paul wrote it in Hebrew and Luke translated into Greek (Eusebius, *History* 6.14.2). Perhaps the majority of Bible teachers and commentators believe the Apostle Paul wrote the Hebrews without attaching his name to it, though his original readers knew him (indicated by passages such as Hebrews 13:18-19 and 13:23-24).

ii. However, many other commentators believe it is unlikely that Paul wrote this book. Dods quotes Farrar: "The writer cites differently from St. Paul; he writes differently; he argues differently; he declaims differently; he constructs and connects his sentences differently; he builds up his paragraphs on a wholly different model... His style is the style of a man who thinks as well as writes in Greek; whereas St. Paul wrote in Greek but thought in Syriac."

iii. F.F. Bruce quoted Calvin on this point: "The manner of teaching and the style sufficiently show that Paul was not the author, and the writer himself confesses in the second chapter (Hebrews 2:3) that he was one of the disciples of the apostles, which is wholly different from the way in which Paul spoke of himself."

iv. The early commentator Tertullian (who wrote in the early 200s) said Barnabas wrote Hebrews, but he offered no support for this statement other than that Barnabas was a Levite (Acts 4:36) and a man of encouragement (Acts 4:36).

v. Martin Luther believed that Apollos wrote the book of Hebrews, because Acts tells us Apollos was eloquent and had a strong command of the Old Testament (Acts 18:24).

vi. Adolf Harnack thought Priscilla (with her husband Aquilla) wrote Hebrews, and it remained anonymous to hide its controversial female authorship. But when the writer to the Hebrews writes of himself in Hebrews 11:32, the masculine grammar of the passage argues against the idea that a woman wrote the letter.

vii. No matter who the human author of Hebrews was, there are indications that it was written fairly early in the New Testament period, probably somewhere around AD 67 to 69. The reference to Timothy (Hebrews 13:23) places it fairly early. The present lack of physical persecution (Hebrews 12:4) puts it fairly early. Finally, the lack of any reference to the destruction of the temple probably puts it before AD 70, when Jerusalem and the second temple were destroyed. Since the writer to the Hebrews was so concerned with the passing of the Old Covenant, it seems unlikely that he would ignore the destruction of the temple if it had already happened before he wrote.

b. **God**: This is how the book begins. There is no attempt to prove God's existence; Scripture assumes we learn of God's existence and some of His attributes from nature (Psalm 19:1-4 and Romans 1:20). The writer of the Hebrews knew that God existed and that He spoke to man.

i. "Deity is not to be explained, but to be adored; and the Sonship of Christ is to be accepted as a truth of revelation, to be apprehended by faith, though it cannot be comprehended by the understanding." (Spurgeon)

c. **Who at various times and in different ways spoke**: The revelation given through the prophets was brought in **various** ways - sometimes through parables, historical narrative, prophetic confrontation, dramatic presentation, psalms, proverbs, and the like.

i. It is true that God spoke in a variety of ways in the Old Testament.

- He spoke to Moses by a burning bush (Exodus 3).

- He spoke to Elijah by a still, small voice (1 Kings 19).

- He spoke to Isaiah by a heavenly vision (Isaiah 6).

- He spoke to Hosea by his family crisis (Hosea 1:2).
- He spoke to Amos by a basket of fruit (Amos 8:1).

ii. Yet the idea here is that the *prophets* spoke to the *fathers* in various ways; not that God spoke to the prophets in various ways (though that is true also).

iii. Using the properties of light as an illustration, we may say that God spoke in a spectrum in the Old Testament. Jesus is a prism that collected all those bands of light and focused them into one pure beam.

iv. This reference to the Old Testament will be repeated often through the Book of Hebrews. Hebrews is a book deeply rooted in the Old Testament. Hebrews has 29 quotations and 53 allusions to the Old Testament, for a total of 82 references. Significantly, Hebrews does not refer even once to the books of the Apocrypha.

d. **These last days**: This term refers to the age of Messiah. It may be a long period, but it is the **last** period.

e. **Spoken to us**: This is the first general mention of the readers, but they are not specifically identified. Yet the context of the work clearly identifies is as a letter - or perhaps even a sermon or an essay - written to Jewish Christians in the first century.

i. The structure of the Book of Hebrews is a different from other New Testament books. It begins like an essay, continues as a sermon and ends like a letter.

ii. Hebrews was obviously written to Christians with a Jewish background, but it was also written to a Greek frame of mind with its analysis of Jesus as the ultimate reality. This approach to the nature of Jesus explains the Savior to the mindset of the Greek philosophers.

iii. Hebrews is basically a book that exhorts discouraged Christians to continue on strong with Jesus in light of the complete superiority of who He is and what He did for us.

f. **Spoken to us by His Son**: It isn't so much that Jesus *brought* a message from the Father; He *is* a message from the Father. The idea is that Jesus is far more than the latest or best prophet. He has revealed something no other prophet could.

i. The revelation from Jesus Himself was unique, because not only was it purely God's message (as was the case with every other inspired writer) but it was also God's *personality* through which the message came. The *personality* of Paul, Peter, John, and other Biblical writers is clear in their writings. Yet in the revelation from Jesus we see the *personality of God.*

ii. The Book of Hebrews (for the most part) does not present Jesus speaking of Himself. There is a sense in which the Son does not speak in Hebrews; the Father speaks concerning the Son. The book of Hebrews is the God the Father telling us what God the Son is all about. "If men cannot learn about God from the Son, no amount of prophetic voices or actions would convince them." (Guthrie)

2. (2b-3) A sevenfold description of the glorious Son.

Whom He has appointed heir of all things, through whom also He made the worlds; who being the brightness of *His* glory and the express image of His person, and upholding all things by the word of His power, when He had by Himself purged our sins, sat down at the right hand of the Majesty on high,

a. **Heir of all things**: This begins a glorious section describing Jesus, first as the **heir of all things**. This is the idea that Jesus is preeminent. It is connected to the Jesus' standing as firstborn over all creation (Colossians 1:15).

b. **He made the worlds**: The ancient Greek word translated **worlds** is *aion*, from which we get our English word "eons." It means that Jesus made more than the material world, He also made the very ages - history itself is the creation of the Son of God.

c. **The brightness of His glory**: Jesus is the **brightness of** the Father's **glory**. The ancient Greek word for **brightness** is *apaugasma*, which speaks of the radiance that shines from a source of light.

i. In this sense, Jesus is the "beam" of God's glory. We have never seen the sun, only the rays of its light as they come to us. Even so, we have never seen the God the Father, but we see Him through the "rays" of the Son of God.

ii. The ancient Greek philosopher Philo used the word *apaugasma* to describe the Logos, the being or intelligent mind who ordered the universe. The writer of Hebrews explained Jesus in terms that made sense to both first-century Jews and those familiar with Greek philosophy.

d. **The express image of His person**: The idea is of an exact likeness as made by a stamp. Jesus *exactly* represents God to us.

e. **Upholding all things by the word of His power**: The idea behind the word translated **upholding** is better thought of as "maintaining." The word does not have the idea of passively holding something up (as the mythical Atlas held up the earth), but of *actively* sustaining.

> i. In His earthly ministry Jesus constantly demonstrated the power of His word. He could heal, forgive, cast out demons, calm nature's fury all at the expression of one word. Here we see that His word is so powerful that it can **uphold all things**.

> ii. "The tense of the verb 'upholding' is significant of Christ's constant work in relation to the world (Colossians 1:17)." (Griffith Thomas)

f. **Himself purged our sins**: From the previous description, we know that the Son of God is a being of great power and wisdom. Now we know He is also a being of great love, who purged the guilt and shame of **our sins**. He did this **Himself**, showing that no one else could do it for us and we could not do it for ourselves.

g. **Sat down at the right hand of the Majesty on high**: This is a position of majesty, of honor, of glory, and of finished work. This position of Jesus sets Him far above all creation.

3. (4) Therefore, Jesus is **so much better than the angels**.

Having become so much better than the angels, as He has by inheritance obtained a more excellent name than they.

a. **Having become so much better than the angels**: This description of Jesus in previous verses shows us that He is far superior than any angelic being. Yet this tells us that Jesus *became* **better than the angels**. We could say that He is *eternally* better than the angels, but He also *became* better than the angels.

> i. Jesus **became** better in the sense that He was made *perfect* (complete as our redeemer) *through sufferings* (Hebrews 2:10) - something no angel ever did.

> ii. Griffith Thomas linked together the descriptions of Jesus given in these first few verses, culminating in Hebrews 1:4:

> - Christ the Heir.
> - Christ the Creator.
> - Christ the Revealer.
> - Christ the Sustainer.
> - Christ the Redeemer.
> - Christ the Ruler.
> - Christ Supreme.

b. **A more excellent name than they**: Jesus' superior status is demonstrated by a superior **name**, which is not merely a title, but a description of His nature and character. There are many reasons why it is important to understand the surpassing excellence of Jesus, setting Him far above every angelic being.

- We often best understand things when they are set in contrast to other things.

- Though the Old Covenant came by the hands of angels to Moses, a better covenant came by a better being, Jesus. First century Jews might think that the gospel came at the hands of mere men - the apostles. But in truth, the gospel came by Jesus, who is superior to the angels.

- There was a dangerous tendency to worship angels developing in the early Church (Colossians 2:18, Galatians 1:8), and Hebrews shows that Jesus is high above any angel.

- There was the heretical idea that Jesus Himself was an angel, a concept that degrades His glory and majesty.

- Understanding how Jesus is better than the angels helps us to understand how He is better than anyone or anything in our life.

    i. In this sense, the purpose of Hebrews is like the purpose of the Transfiguration of Jesus mentioned in the Gospels. They each cry out and say, "*This is My beloved Son. Hear Him!*" (Mark 9:7)

B. The Scriptures prove Jesus is superior to the angels.

1. (5) Jesus is superior to the angels because He is the Son of God, as shown in Psalm 2:7 and 2 Samuel 7:14.

For to which of the angels did He ever say:

"You are My Son,
Today I have begotten You"?

And again:

"I will be to Him a Father,
And He shall be to Me a Son"?

a. **For to which of the angels did He ever say**: The author of Hebrews proved that Jesus is superior to any angelic being because God the Father says things to God the Son that He never said to angels.

    i. "The Jews venerated angels because of their place in the giving of the Law (Acts 7:53; Galatians 3:19), and it was essential that Jewish Christians should learn by this comparison something of the infinite superiority of our Lord over those heavenly beings that held so prominent a place in Jewish life." (Thomas)

ii. Lesser things, if allowed more focus, take a bigger place than the greater and more important things.

iii. **Did He ever say**: The writer to the Hebrews clearly thought that *God* spoke through the human authors of the Old Testament.

b. **You are My Son**: Psalm 2:7 shows that God the Father called Jesus, "**Son**" - the *more excellent name* of Hebrews 1:4. This shows that Jesus is greater than the angels, because no angel was ever given this great name.

i. Though the angels may *collectively* be called "sons of God" (such as in Job 1:6), but no angel is ever given that title *individually*.

c. **Today I have begotten You**: God the Father also spoke to God the Son and described Him as **begotten**. The word **begotten** speaks of the equality of *substance* and *essential nature* between the Father and Son. It means that the Father and the Son share the same *being*.

d. **I will be to Him a Father, and He shall be to Me a Son**: This quotation from 2 Samuel 7:14 is another example of something that God the Father said to God the Son that He never said to any angel.

i. This statement is a good example of an Old Testament prophecy that had two fulfillments in mind. In a near and imperfect sense, the promise of 2 Samuel 7:14 was fulfilled in David's son Solomon. In a more distant and perfect sense, it is fulfilled in the Son of David, Jesus Christ.

2. (6-7) Jesus is superior to the angels because angels worship and serve Jesus, who is their God, as shown in Deuteronomy 32:43 (in the Septuagint and the Dead Sea Scrolls) and Psalm 104:4.

But when He again brings the firstborn into the world, He says:

"Let all the angels of God worship Him."

And of the angels He says:

**"Who makes His angels spirits
And His ministers a flame of fire."**

a. **When He brings the firstborn**: This word was used both as an *idea* and to designate the one born first. Since the firstborn son was "first in line" and received the position of favor and honor, the title "**firstborn**" could indicate that someone was of the highest position and honor.

i. Many of those *not* born first in the Bible are given the title "firstborn." David is an example of this (Psalm 89:27) and so is Ephraim (Jeremiah 31:9).

ii. According to Rabbi Bechai (quoted in Lightfoot) the ancient Rabbis called Yahweh Himself "Firstborn of the World." It was a title, not a description of origin.

iii. Rabbis used **firstborn** as a specifically Messianic title. One ancient Rabbi wrote, "God said, 'As I made Jacob a first-born (Exodus 4:22), so also will I make king Messiah a first-born (Psalm 89:28).'" (R. Nathan in *Shemoth Rabba*, cited in Lightfoot)

b. **Let all the angels of God worship Him**: Deuteronomy 32:43 shows that Jesus is superior because He is the *object* of angelic worship, not an angelic worshipper. The angels worship Him; He does not worship among them. Revelation 5 gives a glimpse of the angelic worship of Jesus.

c. **Who makes His angels spirits and His ministers a flame of fire**: Psalm 104:4 demonstrates that Jesus the Messiah is Lord over the angels. They are *His* angels and *His* ministers. The angels belong to Jesus, and He is not among them.

3. (8-12) Jesus is superior to the angels because the Father Himself calls Him (and not any angel) God and LORD (Yahweh), as shown in Psalm 45:6-7 and 102:25-27 from the Septuagint.

But to the Son *He says:*

"Your throne, O God, *is* forever and ever;
A scepter of righteousness *is* the scepter of Your kingdom.
You have loved righteousness and hated lawlessness;
Therefore God, Your God, has anointed You
With the oil of gladness more than Your companions."

And:

"You, LORD, in the beginning laid the foundation of the earth,
And the heavens are the work of Your hands.
They will perish, but You remain;
And they will all grow old like a garment;
Like a cloak You will fold them up,
And they will be changed.
But You are the same,
And Your years will not fail."

a. **But to the Son He says**: Again, the emphasis is that God the Father says things to God the Son that are never said to angelic beings.

b. **Your throne, O God**: Psalm 45:6-7 plainly says that God the Father calls the Son **God**. When the First Person of the Trinity spoke to the Second Person of the Trinity, He called Him **God**. This is unique and powerful evidence of the deity of Jesus.

i. Some argue that there are many beings called "gods" in the Bible such as Satan (2 Corinthians 4:4) and earthly judges (Psalm 82:1 and 6). But these others are *supposed* gods, *pretenders* to their throne. If Jesus is not the *true* God, He is a *false* god, like Satan and the wicked judges of Psalm 82.

ii. But Jesus *is* the True and Living God, called so here by God the Father; and also by John in John 1:1, by Thomas in John 20:28, and by Paul in Titus 2:13 and Titus 3:4.

c. **Therefore God, Your God, has anointed You**: This passage shows striking interaction between the Persons of the Trinity. "**God, Your God**" speaks of the Father and His position of authority over the Second Person of the Trinity. "**You**" refers to the Son. "**Anointed**" has in mind the ministry and presence of the Holy Spirit, the Third Person of the Trinity.

d. **You, LORD, in the beginning**: Psalm 102:25-27 shows that the Son is not only called **God**, but also **LORD** (Yahweh). Then the Son is described with attributes and terms that belong only to God.

i. **You, LORD, in the beginning laid the foundation of the earth**: This shows that Jesus Christ, the Second Person of the Trinity, is the Creator. Yahweh is specifically said to be the Creator (Isaiah 45:12, Isaiah 45:18).

ii. **They will perish, but You will remain**: This shows that Jesus Christ, the Second Person of the Trinity is self-existent, even as Psalm 102:25-27 says this of Yahweh.

iii. **Like a cloak You will fold them up, and they will be changed**: This shows that Jesus Christ, the Second Person of the Trinity is sovereign, with authority over all creation and history, even as Psalm 102:25-27 says this of Yahweh.

iv. **You are the same**: This shows that Jesus Christ, the Second Person of the Trinity is immutable, unchanging, and eternal (**Your years will not fail**). Psalm 102:25-27 says this of Yahweh and the writer to the Hebrews says that it clearly applies to Jesus as well.

4. (13-14) Jesus is superior to the angels because He sat down, having completed His work, while the angels work on continually, as shown in Psalm 110:1.

But to which of the angels has He ever said:

"Sit at My right hand,
Till I make Your enemies Your footstool"?

Are they not all ministering spirits sent forth to minister for those who will inherit salvation?

a. **But to which of the angels has He ever said**: Now for the seventh time in this chapter, the writer to the Hebrews quotes the Hebrew Scriptures to demonstrate that Jesus the Messiah is far superior to any angelic being. He quoted Psalm 110:1 to show again that God the Father said things to Jesus the Messiah never said to angelic beings.

b. **Sit at My right hand**: Psalm 110:1 says that the Messiah has this exalted placed and posture in heaven. Anyone who sits in the divine presence shows that they have the perfect right to be there. There are no seats for the angels around the throne of God, because they are constantly busy praising God and serving Him. Yet Jesus can - at the invitation of God the Father - **sit** at the **right hand** of God the Father.

i. It isn't good to be too comfortable in the presence of majesty. There is a story about a man named Lear who was hired to give Queen Victoria art lessons. Things went well, and Lear started to feel quite at home in the palace. He enjoyed standing in front of the fire, leaning on the hearth and warming himself in a relaxed manner, but every time he did one of the Queen's attendants invited him to look at something on the other side of the room, making him move. No one explained it to him, but after a while he got the idea: good manners said it was wrong for a subject to have such a relaxed attitude in the presence of their Queen. Jesus is not a subject - He is the Sovereign, so He sits in the presence of majesty.

c. **But to which of the angels has He ever said: "Sit at My right hand."** The angels are not permitted to relax before God. They stand before the Father, but the Son sits down - because He isn't a subject, He is the Sovereign.

d. **Are they not all ministering spirits**: Angels are **ministering spirits**, not *governing* spirits; *service*, not *dominion* is their calling. In this respect angels are like a toy that won't quit. They keep working while the Son takes a posture of rest because He is the Son.

i. Jesus is also called a servant and a minister, but this is part of His voluntary humiliation, not his essential nature - as it is in the essential nature of angels to be servants.

e. **Sent forth to minister for those who will inherit salvation**: The angels are commanded to serve God, but He shares His servants with redeemed men and women. This shows the great love of God for us, and how He wants to share all things with us.

i. Comparing Hebrews 1:2 and 1:14, "It is particularly noteworthy, as bearing on the main theme of the Epistle, that both Christ and Christians are described as heirs." (Thomas)

Hebrews 2 - Jesus, Our Elder Brother

A. Therefore: Because of the superiority of Jesus to the angels, we must pay attention to Jesus.

1. (1) The lesson of the first chapter is applied: listen and don't drift away.

Therefore we must give the more earnest heed to the things we have heard, lest we drift away.

a. **Therefore**: The use of **therefore** in Hebrews makes us pay attention to a point of application after the writer develops a principle. The Scriptural *fact* of Jesus' superiority over the angels has life-changing application - and now we must consider the application.

b. **We must give the more earnest heed**: This is what we must *do* in light of Jesus' superiority over angels. We must give **more earnest heed** to the words of Jesus. It's easy to think this exhortation is directed to unbelievers, but this letter was written to Christians.

i. **Give the more earnest heed**: This has not only the idea of *hearing* carefully, but also in *doing* what we hear - and we ***must*** give the more earnest heed. There is an urgency and necessity to this.

c. **Lest we drift away**: If we do not **give the more earnest heed**, we will **drift away**. The writer had the drifting of a boat in mind, and such drifting happens naturally without an anchor to something solid. If we are not securely set in the truth of the supremacy of Jesus, we will drift into danger with the currents of the world, the flesh, and the devil.

i. The ancient Greek phrase for **drift away** comes from the idea "to slip" (Dodds). It was used for an arrow slipping from the quiver, for snow slipping off a landscape, or of food slipping down the windpipe to cause choking. It happens easily. One doesn't have to *do* anything to **drift away**. Departure from the faith usually comes from slow drifting, not a sudden departure.

ii. The Philippian jailer asked Paul, *What must I do to be saved?* (Acts 16:30) – Paul answered him. The question, *"What must I do to be lost?"* also has an answer: *nothing*. To do *nothing* is to quite enough to be driven by the currents of the world, the flesh, and the devil and to **drift away**.

iii. "The protection against drifting is to have Christ as once the anchor and rudder of life. The anchor will hold us to the truth, while the rudder will guide us by the truth." (Griffith Thomas)

2. (2-4) The lesson emphasized: how shall we escape if we neglect so great a salvation?

For if the word spoken through angels proved steadfast, and every transgression and disobedience received a just reward, how shall we escape if we neglect so great a salvation, which at the first began to be spoken by the Lord, and was confirmed to us by those who heard *Him*, God also bearing witness both with signs and wonders, with various miracles, and gifts of the Holy Spirit, according to His own will?

a. **The word spoken through angels**: This describes the Mosaic Law, which was *received...by the direction of angels* (Acts 7:53). The idea is that the law was delivered in some way to Moses by the hands of angels.

i. The idea that angels had a role in bringing the Law to Moses is found in Deuteronomy 33:2, Acts 7:53, and in Galatians 3:19. Josephus also repeated this idea in his ancient history (*Antiquities*, 15.53).

b. **Proved steadfast**: The Mosaic Law was **steadfast** and strict (**every transgression and disobedience received a just reward**). It demanded to be taken seriously.

c. **How shall we escape**: If we must take the word which came by angels seriously, then we must take the word that came by the *Son of God* even more seriously. The Son is proven to be greater than the angels, so His message should be regarded as greater.

i. A greater *word* brought by a greater *Person* having greater *promises* will bring a greater *condemnation* if it is neglected.

d. **If we neglect so great a salvation**: The ancient Greek word translated **neglect** is *amelesantes*, also used in Matthew 22:5 of those who disregarded the invitation to the marriage supper (*they made light of it*). It means to have the *opportunity*, but to ignore or to disregard the opportunity.

i. This was a word to *believers*, not to those outside the faith. The danger described isn't *rejecting* salvation (though the principle certainly applies there also), but the danger is *neglecting* salvation.

ii. Remember that Hebrews was written not primarily as an evangelistic tract, but as an encouragement and warning to discouraged Christians. It was written to those who neglected an abiding walk with Jesus.

e. **So great a salvation**: When we consider something **great**, we will naturally pay attention to it and not **neglect** it. If we do not consider something great we leave it to convenience rather than to commitment.

i. "The phrase, 'so great salvation,' is a striking reminder of what God has provided in Christ. The word 'so' is similar to the instance in the familiar passage, 'God so loved the world' (John 3:16), and expresses an unfathomable depth." (Griffith Thomas)

ii. Therefore, if we neglect something, we probably do not consider it great. Yet our salvation *is* great, because:

• We are saved by a great Savior.

• We are saved at a great cost.

• We are saved from a great penalty.

iii. A reason many neglect their salvation is because they never see it as salvation. They see it merely as *receiving* something, not as being *rescued* from something.

f. **Spoken by the Lord, and was confirmed**: This word was spoken by Jesus and confirmed by eyewitnesses (**those who heard Him**). Then it was **confirmed** with **signs**, **wonders**, **miracles** and **gifts of the Holy Spirit** given by God.

i. In saying **and was confirmed to us** *by those who heard Him*, the writer shows that he was not a "first generation" Christian. He heard the message second-hand through the apostles and eyewitnesses of Jesus' ministry.

ii. Hebrews 2:3 is one reason some believe the Apostle Paul did not write Hebrews. In other passages, Paul clearly set himself on an equal level with the apostles and other eyewitnesses of Jesus (1 Corinthians 9:1 and 1 Corinthians 15:3-11).

g. **God also bearing witness**: God does confirm His word with **various miracles, and gifts of the Holy Spirit**. But He does it all **according to His own will**, not on the command of man.

i. Jesus said miraculous signs would follow those who believe (Mark 16:17). If there is no element of the miraculous, one may question whether there is true belief in Jesus or if the word of God is truly being preached. The preacher must give God something to confirm.

ii. On the other hand, the Spirit brings such miracles and gifts **according to *His* will**. Miracles can't be "worked up" and brought about by human effort or emotion. Much damage is done by those who don't think *enough* miracles are happening, and want to "prime the pump" with the enthusiasm of the flesh.

iii. It's hard to say which is worse - the denial of miracles and the gifts of the Holy Spirit, or the counterfeit of them. Either error is dangerous.

B. The glorious humanity of Jesus Christ.

1. (5-8a) We know Jesus is human, because God put the world in subjection to man, not angels (quoting from Psalm 8:4-6).

For He has not put the world to come, of which we speak, in subjection to angels. But one testified in a certain place, saying:

**"What is man that You are mindful of him,
Or the son of man that You take care of him?
You have made him a little lower than the angels;
You have crowned him with glory and honor,
And set him over the works of Your hands.
You have put all things in subjection under his feet."**

For in that He put all in subjection under him, He left nothing *that is* not put under him.

a. **He has not put the world to come…in subjection to angels**: God never gave angels the kind of dominion man originally had over the earth (Genesis 1:26-30). Angels do not have dominion over this world or the world to come.

i. "The divine purpose for the world is that man, not angels, is to rule in the future." (Griffith Thomas)

b. **What is man**: The quotation from Psalm 8:4-6 shows both the smallness of man in relation to the God of creation, and the dominion God gave to man, even though he is **a little lower than the angels**.

c. **You have made him a little lower than the angels**: In chapter one, the writer to the Hebrews brilliantly demonstrated from the Scriptures the deity of Jesus and His superiority over all angels. Now he demonstrates the *humanity* of Jesus from the Scriptures and applies the implications of Jesus' humanity.

i. It is Biblically wrong to think of Jesus as merely God or merely man. It is wrong to think of Him as half God and half man (or any other percentage split). It is wrong to think of Him as "man on the outside" and "God on the inside." The Bible teaches Jesus is *fully* God and *fully* man, that a human nature was added to His divine nature, and both natures existed in one Person, Jesus Christ.

ii. Significantly, the first false teaching about Jesus in the days of the early church did not deny that He was God, but it denied that He was really human and said He only *seemed* to be human. The heresy was called *Docetism*, coming from the ancient Greek word "*to seem*," and was taught by Cerinthus, who opposed the apostle John in the city of Ephesus and whose teaching is probably the focus of 1 John 4:2 and 1 John 5:6.

d. **He left nothing that is not put under him**: The writer emphasizes the point that God put *all* things (not *some* things) under subjection to human beings. This shows that Jesus must be human, because God gave this dominion to humans and Jesus exercises this authority.

2. (8b-9) A problem and its solution.

But now we do not yet see all things put under him. But we see Jesus, who was made a little lower than the angels, for the suffering of death crowned with glory and honor, that He, by the grace of God, might taste death for everyone.

a. **But now we do not yet see all things put under him**: By all appearance the promise of Psalm 8:4-6 seems to be unfulfilled. We do not see that all things are subjected to man.

b. **But we see Jesus**: The promise is fulfilled in Jesus, who is Lord over all. Through Jesus, man can regain the dominion originally intended for Adam (Revelation 1:6, 5:10 and Matthew 25:21).

i. There are many things we will not understand until we **see Jesus**. The answers to life's most perplexing questions are not found in asking "Why?" The greatest answer is a *Who* - Jesus Christ.

ii. Some wish they might truly **see Jesus** with their natural eye, instead of the eye of faith. Yet, "Sight is very frequently used in Scripture as a metaphor, an illustration, a symbol, to set forth what faith is. Faith is the eye of the soul. It is the act of looking unto Jesus." (Spurgeon)

iii. Think of how many who saw Jesus with the natural eye resisted Him, mocked Him, rejected Him. It's better to see Jesus with the eye of faith than with the natural eye.

- It does not say, "We can see Jesus" though that is true.
- It does not say, "We have seen Jesus" though that was true of some in his day.
- It does not say, "We shall see Jesus" though that is certainly true.

- It says, **we see Jesus**, both now and continually. He is the focus, the center, the main aspect of our spiritual life.

iv. So, look unto Jesus with the eye of faith – as imperfect as your vision of faith may be, look unto Him who is perfect.

- See Him as the One who loves sinners and died for them.

- See Him as your Savior.

- See Him as your Master.

- See Him as your Friend.

- See Him as your Forerunner.

- See Him as your Healer.

- See Him at home, at work, out and about – not only *here* at worship times.

c. **Who was made a little lower than the angels**: This promise of dominion could only be fulfilled through the humility, suffering, and death of Jesus. The Son of God defeated the evil Adam brought into the world - which was death (Romans 5:12).

i. God gave man dominion over the earth, but man forfeited his power (not his right or authority) to take that dominion through sin, and the principle of death took away the power to rule. But Jesus came and through His humility and suffering He defeated the power of death and made possible the fulfillment of God's promise that humans will have dominion over the earth - fulfilled both through Jesus' own dominion, and the rule of believers with Him (Revelation 20:4).

d. **Made a little lower than the angels, for the suffering of death**: If God the Son did not add humanity to His deity, and in His humanity become **a little lower than the angels**, then He could never experience the **suffering of death** on our behalf.

e. **Crowned with glory and honor, that He, by the grace of God, might taste death for everyone**: This tells us that the **suffering of death** for Jesus was only a prelude to being **crowned with glory and honor**. It also tells us that His death was, in some way, **for everyone**.

3. (10-13) We know Jesus is human, because He calls us **brethren**.

For it was fitting for Him, for whom *are* all things and by whom *are* all things, in bringing many sons to glory, to make the captain of their salvation perfect through sufferings. For both He who sanctifies and those who are being sanctified *are* all of one, for which reason He is not ashamed to call them brethren, saying:

"I will declare Your name to My brethren;
In the midst of the assembly I will sing praise to You."

And again:

"I will put My trust in Him."

And again:

"Here am I and the children whom God has given Me."

a. **For it was fitting**: It was more than necessary - it was **fitting** for the sovereign God - **for whom are all things and by whom are all things** to be made **perfect through sufferings** in the task of **bringing many sons to glory**.

i. Conceivably, God could have engineered a way to save us that did not require the suffering of the Son of God. But **it was fitting** for Jesus to save us at the cost of His own agony.

ii. This is the ultimate illustration of the fact that real love, real giving, involves *sacrifice*. As David said: *nor will I offer... offerings to the LORD my God which costs me nothing* (2 Samuel 24:24). God's love for us had to show itself in sacrifice and God could not sacrifice unless He added humanity to His deity and suffered on our behalf.

b. **The captain of their salvation**: Jesus is the **captain** - the leader, the advance - of our salvation. This has wonderful implications:

- A captain makes all the arrangements for the march, and Jesus makes all the arrangements for our progress as Christians.

- A captain gives the commands to the troops - "Go" or "Stay" or "Do this." Jesus commands us as our captain.

- A captain leads the way and is an example to his men, and Jesus does this for us.

- A captain encourages his men, and Jesus encourages us.

- A captain rewards his troops, and Jesus rewards His followers.

i. "Now, seeing that it is the will of the Lord to lead us to glory by the Captain of our salvation, I want you to be worthy of your Leader. Do you not think that, sometimes, we act as if we had no Captain? We fancy that we have to fight our way to heaven by the might of our own right hand, and by our own skill; but it is not so. If you start before your Captain gives you the order to march, you will have to come back again; and if you try to fight apart from your Captain, you will rue the day." (Spurgeon)

c. **Perfect through sufferings**: There was nothing lacking in the deity of Jesus. Yet until He became a man and suffered, God never *experienced* suffering.

> i. "*To make perfect* does not imply moral imperfection in Jesus, but only the consummation of that human experience of sorrow and pain through which he must pass in order to become the leader of his people's salvation." (Vincent)

> ii. "We know that had he only been God yet still he would not have been fitted for a perfect Savior, unless he had become *man*. Man had sinned; man must suffer. It was man in whom God's purposes had been for a while defeated; it must be in man that God must triumph over his great enemy." (Spurgeon)

> iii. The point is that **it was fitting** for the Father to do this, in the sense that *it pleased the* LORD *to bruise Him* (Isaiah 53:10), to do it for the sake of **bringing many sons to glory**.

d. **For both He who sanctifies and those who are being sanctified *are* all of one**: Therefore we are **sanctified** by One who has been sanctified. We are all of the same human family, so Jesus **is not ashamed to call them** (that is, us) **brethren**. He could not be our brother unless He was also human like us.

> i. **Being sanctified**: "Well, then, dear friends, are you sanctified? I have heard some make a jest of that word, and jeer at certain persons as 'saints.' They might as well call them kings and princes, and then mock at them, for there is nothing mean or despicable in the name 'saint.' It is one of the most glorious titles that a man can ever wear." (Spurgeon)

> ii. It is not remarkable that I am unashamed to associate with Jesus. But it is remarkable that He **is not ashamed to call** us **brethren**.

e. **He is not ashamed to call them brethren, saying**: The writer cites three proofs that Jesus the Messiah calls His people His brethren from Psalm 22:22, Isaiah 8:17, and Isaiah 8:18.

> i. In each of these examples the Messiah is willing to associate Himself with His brethren, whether it be in a congregation of worship, a community of trust in the Father, or declaring a common family association.

f. **In the midst of the assembly I will sing praise to You**: This wonderful quote from Psalm 22:22 (from the ancient Septuagint) reminds us that Jesus sang, singing worship to His Father among His brethren.

i. "Did Jesus sing? Yes, literally. After supper, they sang a hymn. It must have been most thrilling to hear Christ's voice, quivering with emotion, singing the Psalms, which constituted the Great Hallel." (Spurgeon)

ii. "Behold, then, in your midst, O Church of God, in the days of his flesh there stood this glorious One whom angels worship, who is the brightness of his Father's glory in the very heaven of heavens; yet when he stood here, it was to join in the worship of his people, declaring the Father's name unto his brethren, and with them singing praises unto the Most High. Does not this bring him very near to you? Does it not seem as if he might come at any moment, and sit in that pew with you; I feel as if already he stood on this platform side by side with me; why should he not?" (Spurgeon)

g. **Here am I and the children whom God has given Me**: The phrasing of this quote from Isaiah 8:18 shows how precious Jesus' people are to Him. "He likes to dwell on that fact. They are precious to him in themselves, but far more precious as the Father's gift to him. Some things are valued by you as keepsakes given by one you love; and so are we dear to Christ because his Father gave us to him." (Spurgeon)

4. (14-16) What Jesus did as our Brother.

Inasmuch then as the children have partaken of flesh and blood, He Himself likewise shared in the same, that through death He might destroy him who had the power of death, that is, the devil, and release those who through fear of death were all their lifetime subject to bondage. For indeed He does not give aid to angels, but He does give aid to the seed of Abraham.

a. **He Himself likewise shared in the same**: For Jesus to truly fulfill the role of "Elder Brother" for the family of the redeemed, He *had to* take on **flesh and blood**. He had to enter into the prison to free the captives.

b. **Through death He might destroy him who had the power of death, that is, the devil**: Some take this as meaning that Jesus destroyed Satan's "right" to rule over man, which was presumably given to him in the garden of Eden through Adam's rebellion. The idea is that Jesus took away Satan's "right" to rule by allowing Satan to "unlawfully" take Jesus' life on the cross, and Satan's "unlawful" action against Jesus forfeited his right to rule over man. In this thinking, the end result is that the devil has no right over those who come to God through Jesus' work on the cross.

i. Since death only has dominion over those who are born sinners or who have sinned (Romans 5:12), Satan had no "right" to take the life of Jesus, who had never sinned nor was born a sinner - and the devil then committed an "unlawful" murder, according to his nature (John 8:44). Jesus allowed the devil to *bruise His heel* so that He could *bruise his head* (Genesis 3:15).

ii. The problem with this approach is that we know the devil did not *take* Jesus' life. Jesus laid it down of His own accord, and no one took it from Him (John 10:17-18).

iii. However, one might say the devil is guilty of "*attempted* unlawful murder" over someone he had no rights over, because there was no stain of sin on Jesus. Satan certainly *wanted* to murder Jesus and tried to, and Satan is guilty of that.

iv. We know that the devil loves death and murder. "I think death is the devil's masterpiece. With the solitary exception of hell, death is certainly the most Satanic mischief that sin hath accomplished. Nothing ever delighted the heart of the devil so much as when he found that the threatening would be fulfilled, 'In the day that thou eatest thereof thou shalt surely die.'" (Spurgeon)

v. Satan repeatedly tried to kill Jesus. He tried through the murderous intent of Herod when Jesus was a baby. He tried at a synagogue where they tried to kill Jesus. He tried to starve Jesus and tried to drown Him. None of these plans worked, until Jesus stood before Pilate and received the sentence of execution - what joy there was in the counsels of Hell! They were convinced they finally had Jesus where they wanted Him. Yet the death of Jesus became defeat for the devil.

c. **Release those who through fear of death were all their lifetime subject to bondage**: The fear of death rules as a tyrant over humanity. Some try to make peace with death by calling it their friend. But Christians have no fear of death (though perhaps a fear of *dying*), not because death is their friend but because it is a defeated enemy that now serves God's purpose in the believer's life.

d. **He does give aid to the seed of Abraham**: The Father's work in Jesus was not primarily for the sake of angels (though it is for the angels in a secondary sense according to Ephesians 3:10). The work was for the people of faith (**the seed of Abraham**).

i. **Seed of Abraham** is used here in the sense of those who are Abraham's children inwardly, not ethnically (Romans 2:28-29, Galatians 3:7).

5. (17-18) Therefore: Jesus is our faithful High Priest.

Therefore, in all things He had to be made like *His* brethren, that He might be a merciful and faithful High Priest in things *pertaining* to God,

to make propitiation for the sins of the people. For in that He Himself has suffered, being tempted, He is able to aid those who are tempted.

a. **Made like His brethren**: If Jesus were not **like** us He could not be our High Priest, representing us before the Father and making atonement (**propitiation**) for our sins.

i. Neither the Deity nor the Humanity of Jesus is negotiable. If we diminish either then He is unable to save us.

ii. **Propitiation**: "The true idea seems to be…that God offers to Himself the sacrifice of Christ, so that He is at once the One who propitiates and the One who is propitiated." (Griffith Thomas)

b. **That He might be a merciful and faithful High Priest**: The High Priest wore a breastplate with stones engraved with the names of the tribes of Israel on both his chest and his shoulders. The High Priest was therefore in constant sympathy with the people of God, carrying them on his heart and on his shoulders.

i. Jesus did not wear the High Priest's breastplate. But the wound in His chest and the cross on His shoulders are even more eloquent testimony to His heart for us and work on our behalf - **to make propitiation for the sins of the people**.

c. **He Himself has suffered, being tempted**: Some wonder if Jesus was *really* tempted. After all, since He was God (they reason), He could not sin - so His temptation could not be *real*. The writer to the Hebrews insists that not only was Jesus' temptation *real*, but it was so real that He **suffered** under it.

i. We can even say that Jesus' temptation was *more* real and difficult than any we could face. When the pressure of temptation builds, some only find relief by giving into the temptation - *but Jesus never did this*. The pressure of temptation only built and built upon Him.

ii. Jesus knew the temptations of power and the temptations of pain. He knew the temptations of riches and the temptations of poverty. He knew the temptations of popularity and the temptations of rejection. He knew the temptations of the boy and the temptations of the man. He knew temptation from His friends and temptation from His enemies. He knew temptation from His family and temptation from strangers.

iii. "Many persons are tempted, but do not suffer in being tempted. When ungodly men are tempted, the bait is to their taste, and they swallow it greedily. Temptation is a pleasure to them; indeed, they sometimes tempt the devil to tempt them... But good men suffer when they are tempted, and the better they are the more they suffer." (Spurgeon)

d. **He is able to aid those who are being tempted**: Because Jesus added humanity to His deity and experienced human suffering, He is able to help us in temptation. He knows what we are going through.

i. We have two advantages - knowing the *example* of Jesus in temptation, but also having His *active assistance* from heaven, providing strength and a way of escape. With these we can find victory in the midst of temptation and come out *better* from being tempted. Jesus did not lose anything from being tempted - He only gained in glory and sympathy and ability to help His people. In the same way, we do not *have* to lose anything when we are tempted.

ii. "This is the most powerful preservative against despair, and the firmest ground of hope and comfort, that ever believing, penitent sinners could desire or have." (Poole) "Were the rest of the Scripture silent on this subject, this verse might be an ample support for every tempted soul." (Clarke)

iii. "Moreover, *do not make it any cause of complaint that you are tempte*d. If your Lord was tempted, shall the disciple be above his Master, or the servant above his Lord? If the Perfect One must endure temptation, why not you? Accept it, therefore, at the Lord's hands, and do not think it to be a disgrace or a dishonor. It did not disgrace or dishonor your Lord, and temptation will not disgrace or dishonor you. The Lord, who sends it, sends also with it a way of escape, and it will be to your honor and profit to escape by that way." (Spurgeon)

Hebrews 3 - Jesus, Superior to Moses

A. Considering Jesus.

1. (1a) Therefore: who we *are* in light of the previous paragraphs.

Therefore, holy brethren, partakers of the heavenly calling,

a. **Therefore**: From the previous chapter, we are left with the picture of Jesus as our heavenly High Priest. Since this is true, it teaches something about who we are. Understanding who *we are* in light of who Jesus is and what He did is essential for a healthy Christian life. It keeps us from the same depths of discouragement the Hebrew Christians faced.

b. **Holy brethren**: This is who we are because Jesus regards us as such, because our heavenly, holy High Priest is *not ashamed to call them brethren*. (Hebrews 2:11) It should bless and encourage us that Jesus calls us His **holy brethren**.

c. **Partakers of the heavenly calling**: Because Jesus is committed to *bringing many sons to glory* (Hebrews 2:10), we are partners in His heavenly calling. This should bless and encourage us to press on, even through times of difficulty and trial.

2. (1b) Therefore: what we are to *do* in light of the previous paragraphs.

Consider the Apostle and High Priest of our confession, Christ Jesus,

a. **Consider the Apostle**: We don't often apply this word to Jesus, but He is our **Apostle**. The ancient Greek word translated **apostle** really means something like *ambassador*. In this sense, Jesus is the Father's ultimate ambassador (Hebrews 1:1-2). God the Father had to send a message of love that was so important He sent it through **Christ Jesus**.

i. The ancient Greek word translated **consider** is *katanoein*: "It does not mean simply to look at or to notice a thing. Anyone can look at a thing or even notice it without really seeing it. The word means to fix the attention on something in such a way that its inner meaning,

32

the lesson it is designed to teach, may be learned." (Barclay) The same word is used in Luke 12:24 (*Consider the ravens*). It is an earnest appeal to look, to learn, and to understand.

ii. The message is plain: **consider** this. **Consider** that God loves you so much He sent the ultimate Messenger, **Christ Jesus**. **Consider** also how important it is for you to pay attention to God's ultimate **Apostle**, who is **Christ Jesus**.

iii. God also chose His original, authoritative "ambassadors" for the church. These are what we think of as the original twelve apostles. God still chooses ambassadors in a less authoritative sense, and there is a sense in which we are *all* ambassadors for God. Yet surely, Jesus was and is the Father's *ultimate* ambassador.

b. **Consider the... High Priest**: Jesus is the One who supremely represents us before the Father, and who represents the Father to us. God cares for us so much that He put the ultimate mediator, the ultimate **High Priest**, between Himself and sinful man.

i. The message is plain: **consider** this. **Consider** that God loves you so much to give you such a great High Priest. Consider that if such a great **High Priest** is given to us, we must honor and submit to this **High Priest**, who is **Christ Jesus**.

c. **Of our confession**: Jesus is the *ambassador* and the *mediator* of **our confession**. Christianity is a **confession** made with both the mouth and with the life (Matthew 10:32, Romans 10:9).

i. The word "confession" means, "to say the same thing." When we confess our sin, we "say the same" about it that God does. In regard to salvation, all Christians "say the same thing" about their need for salvation and God's provision in Jesus.

3. (2) Consider Jesus as **faithful** in His duties before the Father.

Who was faithful to Him who appointed Him, as Moses also *was faithful* in all His house.

a. **Who was faithful**: When we *consider* the past faithfulness of Jesus, it makes us understand that He will *continue* to be **faithful**. And as He was **faithful** to God the Father (**Him who appointed Him**), so He will be **faithful** to us. This should bless and encourage us.

b. **As Moses also was faithful in all His house**: Moses showed an amazing faithfulness in his ministry; but Jesus showed a *perfect* faithfulness - surpassing even that of Moses.

B. Jesus, superior to Moses.

1. (3a) Jesus has received more glory than Moses did.

For this One has been counted worthy of more glory than Moses,

a. **Moses**: Moses received much glory from God. This is seen in his shining face after spending time with God (Exodus 34:29-35), in his justification before Miriam and Aaron (Numbers 12:6-8), and before the sons of Korah (Numbers 16).

b. **For this One has been counted worthy of more glory than Moses did**: But Jesus received far more glory from the Father, at His baptism (Matthew 3:16-17), at His transfiguration (Mark 9:7), and at His resurrection (Acts 2:26-27 and Acts 2:31-33).

2. (3b-6) Moses the servant, Jesus the Son.

Inasmuch as He who built the house has more honor than the house. For every house is built by someone, but He who built all things *is* God. And Moses indeed *was* faithful in all His house as a servant, for a testimony of those things which would be spoken *afterward*, but Christ as a Son over His own house, whose house we are if we hold fast the confidence and the rejoicing of the hope firm to the end.

a. **Inasmuch as He who built the house has more honor than the house**: Moses was a *member* of the household of God but Jesus is the creator of that **house**, worthy of greater glory.

i. According to Morris, the ancient Rabbis considered Moses to be the greatest man ever, greater than the angels. The writer to the Hebrews does nothing to criticize Moses, but he looks at Moses in his proper relation to Jesus.

b. **Moses indeed was faithful in all His house as a servant... but Christ as a Son over His own house**: Moses was a faithful **servant**, but he was never called a **Son** in the way Jesus is. This shows that Jesus is greater than Moses.

c. **Whose house we are if we hold fast**: We are a part of Jesus' household **if we hold fast**. The writer to the Hebrews is encouraging those who felt like turning back, helping them to **hold fast** by explaining the benefits of continuing on with Jesus.

i. True commitment to Jesus is demonstrated over the long term, not just in an initial burst. We trust that *He who has begun a good work in you will complete it until the day of Jesus Christ* (Philippians 1:6).

ii. **Whose house we are**: 1 Peter 2:4-5 says we are *being built up a spiritual house*. God has a work to build through His people, even as one might build a **house**.

C. The application of the fact of Jesus' superiority to Moses.

1. (7-11) A quotation from Psalm 95:7-11 and its relevance.

Therefore, as the Holy Spirit says:

"Today, if you will hear His voice,
Do not harden your hearts as in the rebellion,
In the day of trial in the wilderness,
Where your fathers tested Me, tried Me,
And saw My works forty years.
Therefore I was angry with that generation,
And said, 'They always go astray in *their* **heart,**
And they have not known My ways.'
So I swore in My wrath,
'They shall not enter My rest.'"

a. **Therefore, as the Holy Spirit says**: The **Spirit** of God (speaking through His Word) told us that Jesus the Messiah is much greater than Moses. This truth should lead someone to action, and now the writer to the Hebrews will encourage those actions.

b. **Do not harden your hearts**: If those who followed Moses were responsible to surrender unto, to trust in, and to persevere in following God's leader, we are much more responsible to do the same with a greater leader, Jesus the Messiah.

i. The point is clear. As the Holy Spirit speaks, we must hear His voice and *not* allow our hearts to become hardened. We hear the Spirit speak in the Scriptures, in the heart of His people, in those He draws to salvation, and by His works.

ii. Just as the Spirit speaks in many ways, there are also several ways we can harden our heart.

• Some harden their hearts by relapsing into their old indifference.

• Some harden their hearts by unbelief.

• Some harden their hearts by asking for more signs.

• Some harden their hearts by presuming upon the mercy of God.

c. **Today**: There is *urgency* to the voice of the Holy Spirit. He never prompts us to get right with God *tomorrow*, or to trust in *yesterday* - the Holy Spirit only moves us to act **today**.

i. The Holy Spirit tells us **today** because it is a *genuine* invitation. We know that the Holy Spirit really wants us to come to Jesus because He says, "**today**." If someone asks me to come over their house for dinner but they give no day or time, I know it isn't a firm invitation yet. But when they say, "Come over on this day at this time," I know it is a *firm* invitation, that they *want* me to come, that they *are ready* for me to come, and that it will be *prepared* for my coming. The Holy Spirit gives you a time for His invitation - **today**.

ii. Charles Spurgeon pointed out one reason why the Holy Spirit is so urgent: "Besides, he waits to execute his favourite office of a Comforter, and he cannot comfort an ungodly soul, he cannot comfort those who harden their hearts. Comfort for unbelievers would be their destruction. As he delights to be the Comforter, and has been sent forth from the Father to act specially in that capacity, that he may comfort the people of God, he watches with longing eyes for broken hearts and contrite spirits, that he may apply the balm of Gilead and heal their wounds."

iii. We must also have great urgency about **today**. "Select the strongest man you know, and suppose that everything in reference to your eternal welfare is to depend upon whether he lives to see the next year. With what anxiety would you hear of his illness, how concerned you would be about his health? Well, sinner, your salvation is risked by you upon your own life, is that any more secure?" (Spurgeon)

d. **As in the rebellion, in the day of trial**: The **day of trial** refers first to the trial at Meribah (Numbers 20:1-13). More generally it speaks of Israel's refusal to trust and enter the Promised Land during the Exodus (Numbers 13:30-14:10). God did not accept their unbelief and He condemned that generation of unbelief to die in the wilderness (Numbers 14:22-23 and 14:28-32).

i. This only makes sense because there is some continuity in God's work among His people through the centuries. We can learn from the mistakes of God's ancient people.

e. **And saw My works forty years**: Because of their unbelief, the people of Israel faced judgment which culminated after **forty years**. This warning in Hebrews was written about **forty years** after the Jews' initial rejection of Jesus. God's wrath was quickly coming upon the Jewish people who rejected Jesus, and would culminate with the Roman destruction of Jerusalem.

f. **Therefore I was angry with that generation**: God's anger was kindled against **that generation** on account of their unbelief. They refused to trust God for the great things He promised, and they were unwilling to continue in trust. Therefore the could not **enter** the **rest** God had appointed for them, the Land of Canaan.

2. (12-15) **Beware**: Don't be like the generation that perished in the wilderness.

Beware, brethren, lest there be in any of you an evil heart of unbelief in departing from the living God; but exhort one another daily, while it is called "Today," lest any of you be hardened through the deceitfulness of sin. For we have become partakers of Christ if we hold the beginning of our confidence steadfast to the end, while it is said:

"Today, if you will hear His voice,
Do not harden your hearts as in the rebellion."

a. **Lest there be in any of you an evil heart of unbelief**: This is strong language, but we often underestimate the terrible nature of our **unbelief**. Refusing to believe God is a serious sin because it shows **an evil heart** and a **departing from the living God**.

i. "Unbelief is not inability to understand, but *unwillingness* to *trust*... it is the will, not the intelligence, that is involved." (Newell)

ii. One can truly believe God, yet be occasionally troubled by doubts. There is a doubt that *wants* God's promise but is weak in faith at the moment. **Unbelief** isn't *weakness* of faith; it sets itself in *opposition* to faith.

iii. "The great sin of not believing in the Lord Jesus Christ is often spoken of very lightly and in a very trifling spirit, as though it were scarcely any sin at all; yet, according to my text, and, indeed, according to the whole tenor of the Scriptures, unbelief is the giving of God the lie, and what can be worse?" (Spurgeon)

iv. "Hearken, O unbeliever, you have said, 'I cannot believe,' but it would be more honest if you had said, 'I *will* not believe.' The mischief lies there. Your unbelief is your fault, not your misfortune. It is a disease, but it is also a crime: it is a terrible source of misery to you, but it is justly so, for it is an atrocious offense against the God of truth." (Spurgeon)

v. "Did I not hear some one say, 'Ah, sir, I have been *trying to believe* for years.' Terrible words! They make the case still worse. Imagine that after I had made a statement, a man should declare that he did not believe me, in fact, he could not believe me though he would like to do so. I should feel aggrieved certainly; but it would make matters worse if he added, 'In fact I have been for years trying to believe you, and I cannot do it.' What does he mean by that? What can he mean but that I am so incorrigibly false, and such a confirmed liar, that though he would like to give me some credit, he really cannot do it? With all the effort he can make in my favour, he finds it quite beyond his power to believe me? Now, a man who says, 'I have been trying to believe in God,' in reality says just that with regard to the Most High." (Spurgeon)

vi. **The living God**: "This divine title is of supreme significance, and shows that God's character is the same to believers as to all else." (Griffith-Thomas)

b. **Exhort one another daily**: If we will strengthen our faith and avoid the ruin of unbelief, we must be around other Christians who will **exhort** - that is, *seriously encourage* us. This shows our responsibility to both *give* exhortation and to *receive* exhortation, and to **exhort one another daily**. It is an easy thing to judge and criticize, but that is not exhortation.

i. If you are out of fellowship altogether, you can't you exhort or be exhorted. When we are out of fellowship there is much less around us to keep us from becoming **hardened through the deceitfulness of sin**.

ii. Some think that Jesus' command to not bother with the speck in our brother's eye while we have a log in our own (Matthew 7:5) indicates that we should not **exhort one another daily**. Yet Jesus told us to *first* deal with our log in our own eye, but *then* to go and deal with the speck in our brother's eye. He did not tell us to ignore their speck, only to deal with it in proper order.

iii. This emphasis on the importance of fellowship stands in the face of society's thinking. A United States survey found that more than 78% of the general public and 70% of churchgoing people believed that "you can be a *good* Christian without attending church." (Roof and McKinney)

iv. "You are to watch over your brethren, to exhort one another daily, especially you who are officers of the church, or who are elderly and experienced. Be upon the watch lest any of your brethren in the church should gradually backslide, or lest any in the congregation should harden into a condition of settled unbelief, and perish in their sin. He who bids you take heed to yourself, would not have you settle down into a selfish care for yourself alone, lest you should become like Cain, who even dared to say to the Lord himself, 'Am I my brother's keeper?'" (Spurgeon)

c. **Lest any of you become hardened**: Christians must be vigilant against hardness of heart. That hidden sin you indulge in - none suspect you of it because you hide it well. You deceive yourself, believing that it really does little harm. You can always ask forgiveness later. You can always die to self and surrender to Jesus in coming months or years. What you cannot see or sense is that your hidden sin hardens your heart. As your heart becomes harder you become *less and less sensitive* to your sin. You become more and more distant from Jesus. And your spiritual danger grows every day.

d. **The deceitfulness of sin**: The sin of unbelief has its root in *deceit* and its flower is marked by *hardness* (**lest any of you be hardened**). Unbelief and sin are **deceitful** because when we don't believe God, we don't stop believing - we simply start believing in a lie.

i. One great danger of sin is its **deceitfulness**. If it came with full revelation, full exposure of all its consequences, it would be unattractive – but the nature of sin is **deceitfulness**.

ii. From the very beginning, much of the power of sin lies in its **deceitfulness**.

- Sin is deceitful in the way that it comes to us.
- Sin is deceitful in what it promises us.
- Sin is deceitful in what it calls itself.
- Sin is deceitful in the excuses it makes, both before and after the sin.

e. **Partakers of Christ**: Believers - those who turn from sin and self and put their life's trust in Jesus - are gloriously called **partakers of Christ**.

i. **Partakers of Christ** - this is the whole picture. Partakers of His obedience, partakers of His suffering, partakers of His death, partakers of His resurrection, partakers of His victory, partakers of His plan, partakers of His power, partakers of His ministry of intercession, partakers of His work, partakers of His glory, partakers of His destiny. Saying "**Partakers of Christ**" says it all.

ii. There are many ways that the believer's union with Jesus is described:

- Like a stone cemented to its foundation.
- Like a vine connected to its branches.
- Like a wife married to her husband.

f. **Do not harden your hearts**: We often say our hearts become hard because of what *others* or *circumstances* do to us. But the fact is that we harden our own hearts in *response* to what happens to us.

3. (16-19) It isn't enough to make a good beginning.

For who, having heard, rebelled? Indeed, *was it* not all who came out of Egypt, *led* by Moses? Now with whom was He angry forty years? *Was it* not with those who sinned, whose corpses fell in the wilderness? And to

whom did He swear that they would not enter His rest, but to those who did not obey? So we see that they could not enter in because of unbelief.

a. **For who, having heard, rebelled?** As a nation, Israel made a good beginning. After all, it took a lot of faith to cross the Red Sea. Yet *all* of that first generation perished in the wilderness, except for the two men of faith - Joshua and Caleb.

i. Think of their great privilege:

- They saw the seven plagues come upon Egypt.
- They had great revelation from God.
- They had received great patience from God.
- They received great mercy.

b. **They would not enter His rest**: 11 times in Hebrews chapters 3 and 4, the Book of Hebrews speaks of *entering rest*. That rest will be deeply detailed in the next chapter. But here, the *key* to entering rest is revealed: *belief*.

c. **So we see that they could not enter in because of unbelief**: One might be tempted to think the key to entering rest is *obedience*, especially from Hebrews 3:18: *to whom did He swear that they would not enter His rest, but to those who did not obey?* But the disobedience mentioned in Hebrews 3:18 is an outgrowth of the **unbelief** mentioned in Hebrews 3:19. The **unbelief** came first, then the disobedience.

i. It was **unbelief** and not something else that kept them out of Canaan:

- Their sin did not keep them out of Canaan.
- Lack of evidence did not keep them out of Canaan.
- Lack of encouragement did not keep them out of Canaan.
- Difficult circumstances did not keep them out of Canaan.

ii. In a New Testament context, our belief centers on the superiority of Jesus Christ, the truth of who He is (fully God and fully man) and His atoning work for us as a faithful High Priest (as in Hebrews 2:17). When we trust in these things, making them the "food" of our souls, we enter into God's rest.

d. **They could not enter in**: Israel's great failure was to persevere in faith. After crossing much of the wilderness trusting in God, and after seeing so many reasons to trust in Him, they end up falling short - because they did not persevere in faith in God and His promise.

i. Jesus reminded us in the parable of the soils with the seeds cast on stony ground and among thorns that it is not enough to make a good beginning, real belief perseveres to the end. It is wonderful to make a good start, but how we finish is even more important than how we start.

ii. C.S. Lewis speaks to the difficulty of persistence (from a tempting demon's fictional perspective): "The Enemy has guarded him from you through the first great wave of temptations. But, if only he can be kept alive, you have time itself for you ally. The long, dull monotonous years of middle-aged prosperity or middle-aged adversity are excellent campaigning weather. You see, it is so hard for these creatures to *persevere*. The routine of adversity, the gradual decay of youthful loves and youthful hopes, the quiet despair (hardly felt as pain) of ever overcoming the chronic temptations with which we have again and again defeated them, the drabness which we create in their lives and inarticulate resentment with which we teach them to respond to it -- all this provides admirable opportunities of wearing out a soul by attrition. If, on the other hand, the middle years from prosperous, our position is even stronger. Prosperity knits a man to the World. He fells that he is 'finding his place in it' while really it is finding its place in him.... That is why we must often wish long life to our patients; seventy years is not a day too much for the difficult task of unraveling their souls from Heaven and building up a firm attachment to the earth." (*The Screwtape Letters*)

iii. If we enter in to God's rest then the coming years will only increase our trust and reliance on Jesus. If by unbelief we fail to enter in, then the coming years will only gradually draw us away from a passionate, trusting relationship with Jesus.

Hebrews 4 - Entering Into His Rest

A. How to enter God's rest.

1. (1-2) The warning is repeated: don't miss God's rest.

Therefore, since a promise remains of entering His rest, let us fear lest any of you seem to have come short of it. For indeed the gospel was preached to us as well as to them; but the word which they heard did not profit them, not being mixed with faith in those who heard *it*.

a. **Therefore**: The idea is carried on without pause from Hebrews 3, that *unbelief* kept the generation that escaped Egypt from entering Canaan. The **promise remains of entering His rest**, and we can enter into that **rest** by faith. *Unbelief* will make us fall short of the **rest** God has for us.

i. The old Puritan commentator John Owen described five features of this **rest** for the believer:

- **Rest** means *peace with God.*
- **Rest** means *freedom from a servile, bondage-like spirit in the worship and service of God.*
- **Rest** means *deliverance from the burden of Mosaic observance.*
- **Rest** means the *freedom of worship according to the gospel.*
- **Rest** means the *rest that God Himself enjoys.*

b. **Let us fear lest any of you seem to have come short of it**: This place of **rest** is so wonderful it should *concern* us when others or we seem to **come short of it**. It isn't enough to *almost* enter His rest; we don't want to **come short** of it.

i. Adam Clarke on **come short**: "It is an allusion, of which there are many in this epistle, to the *races* in the Grecian games: he that *came short* was he who was any distance, no matter how small, *behind* the winner."

42

c. **For indeed the gospel was preached to us as well as to them**: Hearing God's word isn't enough. Ancient Israel **heard** the word but it **did not profit them** because they did not receive it with **faith**. Hearing gave them the opportunity, but the opportunity only profited if it was **mixed with faith**.

d. **Mixed with faith**: One may hear God's word and have spiritual experiences, but unless the work of God is **mixed with faith** it will do no good. This explains why two people can hear the same message and one benefits while the other does not. It also shows that when there is more faith - more of the *anticipation* of blessing and favor from God - there is more blessing indeed.

i. Clarke on **mixed**: "It is a metaphor taken from the nutrition of the human body by mixing the aliment taken into the stomach with the saliva and gastric juice... so that on this process, properly performed, depend (under God) strength, health, and life itself."

ii. Think of the joy Israel had in coming out of Egypt and approaching the Promised Land - and then think of all the graves dug in the desert. A wonderful promise was available but unattained. They came short because though they heard God's word, it was not **mixed with faith**.

2. (3-5) The rest for God's people is like God's own rest.

For we who have believed do enter that rest, as He has said:

"So I swore in My wrath,
'They shall not enter My rest,'"

although the works were finished from the foundation of the world. For He has spoken in a certain place of the seventh *day* in this way: "And God rested on the seventh day from all His works"; and again in this *place*: "They shall not enter My rest."

a. **We who have believed do enter that rest**: This is in contrast to the previously mentioned ones who *did not* enter into God's rest. Unbelief keeps many out of God's rest; faith (**we who have believed**) guides God's people into this **rest**.

b. **My rest**: This quote from Psalm 95:11 demonstrates that this rest is *God's*; it is *His* rest. God finished His work of creation long before Israel came into Egypt or before David wrote Psalm 95 (Genesis 2:2). Yet, although **the works were finished from the foundation of the world**, He still spoke of "**My rest**" – demonstrating that God *still* has this rest.

i. This **rest** is after the pattern of God's own rest **on the seventh day from all His works,** as described in the quote from Genesis 2:2.

ii. **In a certain place** reminds us that ancient scrolls were somewhat unwieldy, and specific passages were not precisely cited according to our more modern tools of chapter and verse.

3. (6-9) The rest that remains for the people of God.

Since therefore it remains that some *must* enter it, and those to whom it was first preached did not enter because of disobedience, again He designates a certain day, saying in David, "Today," after such a long time, as it has been said:

"Today, if you will hear His voice,
Do not harden your hearts."

For if Joshua had given them rest, then He would not afterward have spoken of another day. There remains therefore a rest for the people of God.

a. **Therefore it remains that some must enter it**: God did not create this place of rest in vain. If Israel (**those to whom it was first preached**) failed to enter **because of disobedience**, then someone else would enter into that rest.

b. **Today, if you will hear His voice**: The appeal in Psalm 95:7-8 proves that there is a rest remaining for God's people to enter, beyond the fulfillment under Joshua. If Joshua completely fulfilled the promise of rest, God's appeal through **David**, saying "**Today**" makes no sense.

c. **There remains therefore a rest for the people of God**: All this together proves the point that there is a **rest for the people of God**. This is a **rest** that is spiritual, yet patterned after the rest provided for Israel through Joshua.

i. The mention of **Joshua** reminds us that the name "Jesus" is the same as "**Joshua**." The second Joshua will finish what the first Joshua left unfinished. Jesus is greater than both Moses and the second Joshua.

ii. This rest is in a *person* - in Jesus Christ, more than in doctrines and ideas. If you meet a troubled, crying child and try to comfort them and give them rest using ideas and logic, it won't do much good. But when mommy comes, the child is happy again.

iii. Those who *preach* this rest must *possess* it themselves. "Not long ago, one of our ministers was preaching upon salvation, and the work of the Spirit in the heart, when one of the congregation rose and asked him respectfully, 'Sir, do you know all this by the report of others, or has this taken place in your own experience?' The preacher was by no means put about by the question, but rather rejoiced in it; for he could honestly reply, 'I have trusted Christ. I am saved, and I know and feel the peace which results there from.' If he could not have made that solemn statement, he would have had no influence over the person who had put the question." (Spurgeon)

4. (10) Rest means to not continue on in works.

For he who has entered His rest has himself also ceased from his works as God *did* from His.

a. **He who has entered His rest has himself also ceased from his works**: Entering this rest means no longer needing to *work*. The idea isn't that there is no longer any place for *doing* good **works**. The idea is that there is no longer any place for **works** as a basis for our own righteousness.

i. "There is a sense in which to enter Christian salvation means to cease from one's works and rest securely on what Christ has done." (Morris)

b. **Ceased from his works as God did from His**: This cessation from works as a basis for righteousness fulfills our "Sabbath rest." God rested from His works on the original Sabbath of Genesis 2:2 because the work was finished. We cease from self-justifying works because Jesus finished the work on the cross.

5. (11) Applying the idea and the invitation to enter God's rest through faith.

Let us therefore be diligent to enter that rest, lest anyone fall according to the same example of disobedience.

a. **Let us therefore**: This phrase, or this idea, appears repeatedly in the Book of Hebrews. A doctrinal truth is presented - in this case, the truth of a remaining rest available by faith - then the truth is applied.

b. **Be diligent to enter that rest**: The **rest** is there, but God does not force it upon us. We must **enter that rest**. Clearly, the rest is entered by *faith*; but it takes **diligent** faith. This shows us that faith is not *passive*; it takes *diligence* to trust in, rely on, and cling to Jesus and His work for us.

c. **Lest anyone fall according to the same example of disobedience**: If we are not **diligent to enter that rest**, the result can be a disaster. We may **fall according to the same example of disobedience**. We may **fall**, even as the children of Israel did in the wilderness.

6. (12-13) Found out by God's Word.

For the word of God *is* living and powerful, and sharper than any two-edged sword, piercing even to the division of soul and spirit, and of joints and marrow, and is a discerner of the thoughts and intents of the heart. And there is no creature hidden from His sight, but all things *are* naked and open to the eyes of Him to whom we *must give* account.

a. **For the word of God**: God's Word diagnoses the condition of man with a surgeon's precision. It lays open the heart and accurately discerns spiritual health. In the case of those the writer to the Hebrews first addressed, they were too ready to follow in the failure of the children of Israel and to give up strong, living faith.

b. **Living and powerful**: When the **word of God** exposes our weakness and unbelief like this, it demonstrates its inherent power, sharpness, and accuracy. It bears constant reminding that as we submit ourselves to the **word of God**, we do it for far, far more than intellectual knowledge or to learn Bible facts. We do it for the *ministry of the Word*, because God *meets us* in His Word and the *Holy Spirit* works powerfully through the **word of God**. This spiritual work of God's Word goes far beyond the basic educational value of learning the Bible.

> i. God's word brings true health, fruitfulness, prosperity and success to what we do. (Psalm 1:3)

> ii. The word of God has healing power and the power to deliver from oppression. (Psalm 107:20, Matthew 8:8, Matthew 8:16)

> iii. God's word cleans us. If we take heed according to God's word, our way will be cleansed. (Psalm 119:9, John 15:3, Ephesians 5:26)

> iv. The word of God, hidden in our hearts, keeps us from sin. (Psalm 119:11)

> v. God's word is a counselor. When we delight in God's word, it becomes a rich source of counsel and guidance for us. (Psalm 119:24)

> vi. God's word is a source of strength. (Psalm 119:28)

> vii. God's word imparts life. It is a continual source of life. (Psalm 119:93, Matthew 4:4)

> viii. God's word is a source of illumination and guidance. When God's word comes in, light comes in. It makes the simple wise and understanding. (Psalm 119:105, Psalm 119:130)

> ix. God's word gives peace to those who love it. They are secure, standing in a safe place. (Psalm 119:165)

> x. When the word of God is heard and understood, it bears fruit. (Matthew 13:23)

> xi. The word of God has inherent power and authority against demonic powers. (Luke 4:36)

> xii. Jesus Himself - His eternal person - is described as the *Word*. When we are into the word of God, we are into Jesus. (John 1:1)

xiii. Hearing God's Word is essential to eternal life. One cannot pass from death into life unless they hear the word of God. (John 5:24, James 1:21, 1 Peter 1:23)

xiv. Abiding - living in - God's word is evidence of true discipleship. (John 8:31)

xv. God's word is the means to sanctification. (John 17:17)

xvi. The Holy Spirit can work with great power as the word of God is preached. (Acts 10:44)

xvii. Hearing God's word builds faith. (Romans 10:17)

xviii. Holding fast to the word of God gives assurance of salvation. (1 Corinthians 15:2)

xix. The faithful handling of the word of God gives the ministers of the word a clear conscience. They know that they did all they could before God. (2 Corinthians 4:2, Philippians 2:16)

xx. The word of God is the sword of the Spirit. It is equipment for spiritual battle, especially in the idea of an offensive weapon. (Ephesians 6:17)

xxi. The word of God comes with the power of the Holy Spirit, with "much assurance." (1 Thessalonians 1:5)

xxii. The word of God works effectively in those who believe. (1 Thessalonians 2:13)

xxiii. The word of God sanctifies the very food we eat! (1 Timothy 4:5)

xxiv. The word of God is not dead; it is living and active and sharper than any two edged sword. The word of God can probe us like a surgeon's expert scalpel, cutting away what needs to be cut and keeping what needs to be kept. (Hebrews 4:12)

xxv. The word of God is the Christian's source of spiritual growth. (1 Peter 2:2, 1 Corinthians 2:1-5)

c. **Is living and powerful**: Understanding this spiritual nature of the Bible, the writer to the Hebrews could confidently write this. The Bible isn't a collection of merely old stories and myths. It has *inherent* life and power. The preacher doesn't make the Bible come alive. The Bible *is* alive, and gives life to the preacher and anyone else who will receives it with faith.

i. **Powerful** (translated *active* in the KJV) reminds us that something may be *alive*, yet *dormant*. But God's word is both **living** and **powerful**, in the sense of being *active*.

d. **Sharper than any two-edged sword, piercing even to the division of soul and spirit, and of joints and marrow**: God's word reaches us with surprising precision, and the Holy Spirit empowers the ministry of the word to work deeply in our hearts.

i. Often people wonder how a preacher's message can be *so relevant* to their life. They sometimes honestly wonder if the preacher has secret information about their life. But it isn't necessarily the preacher at all. It is the sharpness of the Word of God, delivering the message in just the right place.

ii. "A sword with two edges has no blunt side: it cuts both this way and that. The revelation of God given us in Holy Scripture is edge all over. It is alive in every part, and in every part keen to cut the conscience, and wound the heart. Depend upon it, there is not a superfluous verse in the Bible, nor a chapter which is useless." (Spurgeon)

iii. "While it has an edge like a sword, it has also a point like a rapier, 'Piercing even to the dividing asunder of soul and spirit.' The difficulty with some men's hearts is to get at them. In fact, there is no spiritually penetrating the heart of any natural man except by this piercing instrument, the Word of God. But the rapier of revelation will go through anything." (Spurgeon)

e. **Even to the division of soul and spirit**: The writer to the Hebrews makes a distinction between **soul** and **spirit**, indicating that a **division** can be made between them.

i. Certainly, there is *some* distinction between **soul** and **spirit**. "The New Testament use of *pneuma* for the human spirit focuses on the spiritual aspect of man, *i.e.* his life in relation to God, whereas *psyche* refers to man's life irrespective of his spiritual experience, *i.e.* his life in relation to himself, his emotions and thought. There is a strong antithesis between the two in the theology of Paul." (Guthrie)

ii. But the stress of this passage isn't to spell out a theology of the difference between **soul** and **spirit**. "Attempts to explain [these terms] on any psychological basis are futile. The form of expression is poetical, and signifies that the word penetrates to the inmost recesses of our spiritual being as a sword cuts through the joints and marrow of our body." (Vincent)

iii. However, it is important to understand what the Bible means with the terms **soul and spirit**. The Bible tells us that people have an "inner" and an "outer" nature (Genesis 2:7, 2 Corinthians 4:16). The inner man is described by both the terms *spirit* (Acts 7:59, Matthew 26:41,

John 4:23-24) and *soul* (1 Peter 2:11, Hebrews 6:19, Hebrews 10:39). These two terms are often used the same way, as a general reference to the inner man. But this is not always the case. Sometimes a distinction is made between **soul and spirit**. We can say that **soul** seems to focus more on *individuality* regarding the inner life (often defined as *the mind, the will, and the emotions*). The **spirit** seems to focus more on supernatural contact and power in the inner life.

iv. That there is *some* distinction between **soul and spirit** is obvious in passages like this (Hebrews 4:12) and 1 Thessalonians 5:23. Passages like Job 7:11 and Isaiah 26:9 show that the terms are *sometimes* both used to generally refer to the inner man.

v. Because the soul and spirit both have reference to the "inner man," they are easily confused. Often an experience intended to build up the **spirit** only "blesses" the **soul**. There is nothing wrong with "soulish" excitement and blessing, but there is nothing in it that builds us up spiritually. This is why many Christians go from one exciting experience to another but never really grow **spirit**ually - the ministry they receive is "**soul**ish." This is why the Word of God is so powerful and precise; it can pierce **even to the division of soul and spirit**, which isn't easy to do.

vi. "When the *soul* is thus distinguished from the *spirit*, by the former is meant that *inferior faculty* by which we *think of* and *desire* what concerns our *present being* and *welfare*. By *spirit* is meant a *superior power* by which we *prefer future things* to *present*." (Clarke)

vii. The terms *flesh* (Colossians 2:5, Matthew 26:41, Galatians 5:16-17) and *body* (Romans 6:6, Romans 8:13, 1 Corinthians 6:13 and 6:19-20) describe the *outer* man. The terms *flesh* and *body* also seem to include aspects of our person such as the senses and habits. When we allow our flesh to direct our thoughts and actions, it ends in spiritual ruin. God wants us to be directed not by the **spirit**, not by the *flesh*, or even the **soul**.

f. **All things are naked and open to the eyes of Him to whom we must give account**: There is no one hidden before God. He sees our heart and knows how to touch it, and we must **give account** for how we respond to His touch.

i. **Naked** reminds us of the way God saw through Adam's feeble hiding. God sees through our hiding the same way.

ii. **Open** translates the ancient Greek word *trachelizo*, used only here in the New Testament. It was used of wrestlers who had a hold that involved gripping the neck and was so powerful that it brought victory. So the word can mean "to prostrate" or "to overthrow;" but many scholars do adopt the simply meaning of "open" - in the sense of laying an opponent open and overcome.

iii. Remember the context. The writer to the Hebrews trusts that he has pierced the hearts of his audience, who thought about "giving up" on Jesus. In this passage, he makes it clear that they can't give up on Jesus can keep it "hidden" from God. The word of God discovers and exposes their condition.

B. Jesus our High Priest.

1. (14) Seeing Jesus, our great High Priest.

Seeing then that we have a great High Priest who has passed through the heavens, Jesus the Son of God, let us hold fast *our* confession.

a. **Seeing then that we have a great High Priest**: The idea that Jesus is our **High Priest** was mentioned before (Hebrews 2:17 and Hebrews 3:1). But now the idea will be developed more extensively.

b. **Seeing then**: The writer to the Hebrews calls attention to the specific, unique character of Jesus as our **High Priest**.

- No other High Priest was called **great**.
- No other **High Priest... passed through the heavens**.
- No other **High Priest** is the **Son of God**.

c. **Let us hold fast our confession**: It is wonderful to know we have a **High Priest**, and how unique and glorious He is. It is even greater to know He **passed through the heavens**, that He ascended into heaven, and now ministers there for our sake. Both these truths should encourage us to **hold fast our confession**.

2. (15) Our High Priest can sympathize with us.

For we do not have a High Priest who cannot sympathize with our weaknesses, but was in all *points* tempted as *we are, yet* without sin.

a. **We do not have a High Priest who cannot sympathize**: Thus far the writer to the Hebrews was careful to document both the deity of Jesus (Hebrews 1:4-14), while careful to also remember His compassionate humanity (Hebrews 2:5-18). It means that Jesus, God the Son, enthroned in heaven, our **High Priest**, can **sympathize with our weaknesses**.

i. To the ancient Greeks, the primary attribute of God was *apatheia*, the essential *inability* to feel anything at all. Jesus isn't like that. He knows and He feels what we go through. The ancient Greek word translated **sympathize** literally means "to suffer along with."

ii. What makes the difference is that Jesus added humanity to His deity, and lived among us. When you have been there, it makes all the difference. We might hear of some tragedy at a high school, and feel a measure of sorrow. But it is nothing like the pain we would feel if it were the high school we attended.

b. **But was in all points tempted as we are, yet without sin**: Jesus knows what it is like to be **tempted** and to battle against sin, though He was never stained by sin. "His sinlessness was, at least in part, an earned sinlessness as he gained victory after victory in the constant battle with temptation that life in this world entails." (Morris)

i. Sometimes we think that because Jesus is God, He could never know temptation the way we do. In part, this is true: Jesus faced temptation much more severely than we ever have or ever will. The Sinless One knows temptation in ways we don't, because only the one who never gives into temptation knows the full strength of temptation. It is true that Jesus never faced temptation in an *inner* sense the way we do, because there was never a sinful nature pulling Him to sin from the *inside*. But He knew the strength and fury of *external* temptation in a way and to a degree that we can never know. He knows what we go through and He has faced worse.

ii. "Yet He endured triumphantly every form of testing that man could endure, without any weakening of His faith in God or any relaxation of His obedience to Him. Such endurance involves more, not less, than ordinary human suffering." (Bruce)

c. **Sympathize with our weaknesses, but was in all points tempted**: Jesus can sympathize with our *weakness* and our *temptation*, but He cannot sympathize with our *sin*. We should not think that this makes Jesus less sympathetic to us, and that He could understand us better if He had sinned Himself.

i. "But listen to me; do not imagine that if the Lord Jesus had sinned he would have been any more tender toward you; for *sin is always of a hardening nature*. If the Christ of God could have sinned, he would have lost the perfection of his sympathetic nature." (Spurgeon)

3. (16) An invitation: come to the throne of grace.

Let us therefore come boldly to the throne of grace, that we may obtain mercy and find grace to help in time of need.

a. **Let us therefore come boldly**: Because we have a High Priest who is both omnipotent and compassionate, we can **come boldly** to His throne. Discouraging us from this access is a central strategy of Satan. The devil sometimes wants us to consider Jesus as unapproachable - perhaps encouraging us to come by Mary or by the saints instead of Jesus. Sometimes the devil wants us to think of Jesus as being powerless to help, not as one who sits on a throne in heaven.

i. Boldly does not mean proudly, arrogantly, or with presumption.

- Boldly means we may come *constantly*.
- Boldly means we may come *without reservation*.
- Boldly means we can come freely, *without fancy words*.
- Boldly means we can come with *confidence*.
- Boldly means we should come with *persistence*.

b. **The throne of grace**: The throne of God is a **throne of grace**. When we come, we may **obtain mercy** (this is *not getting* what we deserve) **and find grace** (this is *getting* what we don't deserve) in our **time of need**.

i. Ancient Jewish Rabbis taught that God had two thrones, one of mercy and one of judgment. They said this because they knew that God was both merciful and just, but they could not reconcile these two attributes of God. They thought that perhaps God had two thrones to display the two aspects of His character. On one throne He showed judgment and on the other throne mercy. But here, in light of the finished work of Jesus, we see mercy and judgment reconciled into one **throne of grace**.

ii. Remember that grace does not *ignore* God's justice; it operates in *fulfillment* of God's justice, in light of the cross.

c. **Find grace to help in time of need**: Thankfully, God provides **help** in our time of need. No request is too small, because He wants us to *be anxious for nothing, but in everything by prayer... let your requests be made known to God*. (Philippians 4:6)

Hebrews 5 - Jesus, A Priest Forever

A. Our Compassionate High Priest.

1. (1-4) Principles of priesthood under the Law of Moses.

For every high priest taken from among men is appointed for men in things *pertaining* to God, that he may offer both gifts and sacrifices for sins. He can have compassion on those who are ignorant and going astray, since he himself is also subject to weakness. Because of this he is required as for the people, so also for himself, to offer *sacrifices* for sins. And no man takes this honor to himself, but he who is called by God, just as Aaron *was.*

a. **For every high priest taken from among men**: God established both the priesthood and the office of high priest in the days of Moses, as described in Exodus 28 and following. The writer to the Hebrews neatly summarizes the work of the **high priest**, in saying "**that he may offer both gifts and sacrifices for sins.**" The primary job of the **high priest** was to officiate, either directly or indirectly through lower-ranking priests, sacrifices unto the Lord.

i. The phrase "**gifts and sacrifices for sins**" reminds us that not every sacrifice offered a blood atonement for sin. Many of the ritual sacrifices were intended as simple gifts to God, expressing thanks and desiring fellowship.

b. **He can have compassion**: Ideally, the **high priest** was more than a meat-cutter offering animals for sacrifice. He also had **compassion on those who are ignorant and going astray**, and ministered the atoning sacrifices with a loving heart for the people. In this ideal, the **high priest** had this **compassion** because he understood that **he himself is also subject to weakness**.

i. God made specific commands to help the **high priest** to minister with compassion. In the breastplate of the **high priest** were set twelve stones engraved with the names of the tribes of Israel, and on the shoulder straps were stones engraved with the names of the tribes. In this, the people of Israel were always on the *heart* and on the *shoulders* of the **high priest** (Exodus 28:4-30). The intention was to stir the compassion of the high priest.

c. **Because of this he is required as for the people, so also for himself, to offer sacrifices for sins**: God also made specific commands to help the **high priest** serve knowing that he was **also subject to weakness**. On the Day of Atonement, the **high priest** had to sacrifice for himself first, to remind he and the nation that he had sin to atone for, just like the rest of the people of Israel (Leviticus 16:1-6).

d. **And no man takes this honor to himself, but he who is called by God, just as Aaron was**: The High Priest was taken *from* the community of God's people but was not *chosen* by God's people. He was appointed by God *for* His people. The principle is that **no man takes this honor to himself**. The office of high priest was nothing to aspire to or campaign for. It was given by right of birth, and therefore chosen by God. It was an honor no man could *take* to himself.

i. The true priesthood and **high priest** came from a specific line of descent. Every priest came from Jacob, Abraham's grandson, whose name was changed to Israel. Every priest came from Levi, one of Israel's twelve sons. God set the tribe of Levi apart as a tribe to serve Him and represent Him to the whole nation of Israel (Exodus 13:2 and Numbers 3:40-41). Levi had three sons: Gershon, Kohath and Merari. Each of these family lines had their own duties. The family of Gershon had care of the tabernacle's screen (veil), fence, and curtains (Numbers 3:25-26). The family of Kohath had care of the tabernacle's furnishings, such as the lampstand, altar of incense, and the ark of the covenant (Numbers 3:31-32). The family of Merari had care of the boards and pillars of the tabernacle and the fence (Numbers 3:36-37). These families were not properly *priests*, though they were *Levites*. The priesthood itself came through Aaron, the brother of Moses, of the family of Kohath. Aaron's family and their descendants made up the priests and the high priest, those able to serve in the tabernacle itself and to offer sacrifice to God. The high priest was generally the eldest son of Aaron, except if they disqualified themselves by sin (as Nadab and Abihu in Leviticus 10:1-3) or according to the regulations of Leviticus 21. In this sense, the priesthood was not popularly elected but chosen by God. Man did not appoint the high priest.

ii. There are dreadful cases where men who were not priests presumed to act as priests. These include:

- Korah, who was swallowed up in a divine earthquake (Numbers 16).

- Saul, who was rejected from his place as king (1 Samuel 13).

- Uzziah, who was struck with leprosy in the temple itself (2 Chronicles 26:16).

iii. Today, we also are prohibited from being our own priest. It is great arrogance to think we can approach God on our own, without a priest. But it is also great superstition to think we need any priest other than Jesus Christ Himself. God provides Jesus as a mediator and priest, and we *must* use the priest God provides.

iv. "A sinner can undertake to manage nothing towards God immediately, or by himself, but with a mediating priest, who must know God's mind and perform it... The common sense of mankind about it since the fall doth evidence it; no nation being without a religion, a temple, a place of worship, or a priest." (Poole)

2. (5-6) Jesus is qualified to be our High Priest.

So also Christ did not glorify Himself to become High Priest, *but it* was He who said to Him:

**"You are My Son,
Today I have begotten You."**

As *He* also *says* in another *place:*

**"You *are* a priest forever
According to the order of Melchizedek";**

a. **Christ did not glorify Himself to become High Priest**: Jesus did not make Himself High Priest. Instead, just as much as Jesus was declared to be the **Son** (in Psalm 2:7), He was also declared to be **a priest forever** (in Psalm 110:4).

i. It is easy to see why the priesthood of Jesus was difficult for early Jewish Christians to grasp. Jesus was not from the lineage of Aaron. Jesus neither claimed nor practiced special ministry in the temple. He *confronted* the religious structure instead of *joining* it. In Jesus' day, the priesthood became a corrupt institution. The office was gained through intrigue and politicking among corrupt leaders.

b. **Today I have begotten You**: This refers to Jesus' resurrection from the dead. At that time He fully assumed His role as our great High Priest, *having been perfected* (Hebrews 5:9).

i. Jesus' resurrection demonstrated that He was not a priest like Aaron, who had to atone for his own sin first. The resurrection vindicated Jesus as the Father's *Holy One* (Acts 2:24 and Acts 2:27), who bore the wrath sinners deserved without becoming a sinner Himself.

c. **A priest forever**: This is an important contrast. Jesus' priesthood (like Melchizedek's) is unending, but no High Priest descended from Aaron ever had a **forever** priesthood.

i. Hebrews 7 will more fully develop the theme of Jesus as a High Priest **according to the order of Melchizedek**.

3. (7-8) The compassion of Jesus, our High Priest.

Who, in the days of His flesh, when He had offered up prayers and supplications, with vehement cries and tears to Him who was able to save Him from death, and was heard because of His godly fear, though He was a Son, *yet* **He learned obedience by the things which He suffered.**

a. **When He had offered up prayers and supplications, with vehement cries and tears**: The agony of Jesus in the Garden of Gesthemane (Matthew 26:36-39, Luke 22:44) proved He struggled with the difficulty of obedience, yet He obeyed perfectly.

i. These prayers were "Most ardent requests, uttered with deep sighs, hands lifted up, and manifold moans, in a most submissive manner." (Trapp)

ii. This answers the question, "How can this glorious, enthroned Jesus know what I am going through down here?" He knows; obedience did not always come easy for Jesus.

b. **Prayers and supplications**: The ancient Greek word for **supplications** is *hiketeria*. This word means "an olive branch wrapped in wool" (Clarke) because that is what the ancient Greek worshipper held and waved to express their desperate prayer and desire. Significantly, this supplication of Jesus took place in a garden of olives - and He supplied the "wool," being the Lamb of God.

c. **And was heard because of His godly fear**: Jesus asked that the cup be taken away from Him (Luke 22:42), yet the cup was not taken away. Nevertheless, His prayer **was heard** because His prayer was not to escape His Father's will, but to *accept* it - and that prayer was definitely heard.

d. **He learned obedience by the things which He suffered**: Though Jesus was God and is God, yet He **learned obedience**. God, enthroned in heaven's glory, can only *experience* **obedience** by casting off the glory of the throne and humbling Himself as Jesus did.

i. Jesus did not pass from disobedience to **obedience**. He learned **obedience** by actually obeying. Jesus did not learn *how* to obey; He learned what is involved in obedience. Jesus learned the *experience* of obedience, and He part of that learning was enduring suffering.

ii. One thing that God, enthroned in heaven does not know is the *experience* of obedience. Enthroned in the heavens, God obeys no one – all obey Him. The angels must have marveled as they saw God the Son, who added humanity to His deity, actually *live out obedience*.

- He obeyed in the spectacular challenges.

- He obeyed in ordinary life.

- He obeyed as a child, as a teen, as a young man.

- He obeyed privately and He obeyed secretly.

- He obeyed God His Father, and He obeyed rightful human authority.

- Jesus obeyed in all things, even to the end.

iii. "Obedience is a trade to which a man must be apprenticed until he has learned it, for it is not to be known in any other way. Even our blessed Lord could not have fully learned obedience by the observation in others of such an obedience as he had personally to render, for there was no one from whom he could thus learn." (Spurgeon)

e. **He learned obedience by things which He suffered**: Suffering was used to teach Jesus. If suffering was good enough to teach the Son of God, we must never despise it as a tool of instruction in our life.

i. Some say that we *might* learn through suffering; but such lessons are only God's second best and God really intends for us to learn only by His word, and it is never His real plan to teach us through trials and suffering. But Jesus was never in the Father's *second best*.

ii. The Bible never teaches that strong faith will keep a Christian from all suffering. Christians are appointed to affliction (1 Thessalonians 3:3). It is through many tribulations we enter the kingdom of God (Acts 14:22). Our present suffering is the prelude to glorification (Romans 8:17).

4. (9-11a) Jesus, our perfected Savior.

And having been perfected, He became the author of eternal salvation to all who obey Him, called by God as High Priest "according to the order of Melchizedek," of whom we have much to say,

a. **Having been perfected, He became the author of eternal salvation**: Jesus' experience of suffering - and subsequent resurrection - made Him perfectly suited to be the **author** (the source, the cause) of our salvation.

i. Sometimes when a person dies and leaves an inheritance, it never gets to the intended heirs. Jesus died leaving an inheritance, and He ever lives to make sure His people receive it. "He died, and so made the legacy good; he rose again and lives to see that none shall rob any one of his beloved of the portion he has left." (Spurgeon)

ii. Some don't want Jesus to be the **author** of their salvation. They want to write their own book of salvation - but God won't read it. Only Jesus can **author** your eternal salvation.

b. **The author of eternal salvation to all who obey Him**: This salvation is extended to **all who obey Him**. In this sense, **all who obey Him** is used to describe those who believe on Him - which simply assumes that believers will obey.

c. **Called by God as High Priest "according to the order of Melchizedek"**: The emphasis is repeated. Jesus is a **High Priest**, who was **called by God** (not by personal ambition), according to the order of **Melchizedek**. The **much to say** comes in Hebrews 7.

B. An exhortation to maturity.

1. (11b) Their dullness of hearing is exposed.

And hard to explain, since you have become dull of hearing.

a. **Since you have become dull of hearing**: This explains why the writer didn't go deeper into the topic of Melchizedek right away. He wanted to address some critical basics before going on to more intricate topics, but their spiritual condition made it **hard to explain**.

i. He feared the discussion of Aaron and Melchizedek and Jesus would sound too academic and theoretical to his readers. At the same time, he recognized this said more about his **dull** *hearers* than it did about the *message*. It wasn't that the message was too complicated; it was that the hearers were **dull of hearing**.

ii. Being **dull of hearing** is not a problem with the ears, but a problem with the heart. The hearer isn't really interested in what God has to say. Not wanting to hear the Word of God points to a genuine spiritual problem. It can even be a reason for unanswered prayer, according to Proverbs 28:9: *One who turns away his ear from hearing the law, even his prayer is an abomination.*

iii. These Christians who felt like giving up with Jesus were also **dull of hearing**. The dullness usually comes first, then the desire to give up. When the Word of God starts to seem dull, we should regard it as a serious warning sign.

b. **You have become dull of hearing**: The word "**become**" is important. It indicates that they didn't start out that **dull of hearing**, but *became* that way. Therefore the writer to the Hebrews *warns* them again.

i. Hebrews is a book filled with warnings. These discouraged Christians need to be encouraged and comforted and taught, but they also needed to be *warned*. They need to be reminded of the consequences of departing from Jesus.

2. (12a) Their failure to mature is exposed.

For though by this time you ought to be teachers, you need *someone* to teach you again the first principles of the oracles of God;

a. **By this time**: According to the time they had been followers of Jesus, they should have been much more mature than they were.

b. **You ought to be teachers**: It wasn't that these were unique people who should hold a unique role of teaching. Instead, they **ought to be teachers** in the sense that every Christian should be a teacher.

i. There is an important sense in which every Christian must be a teacher, because we can all help disciple others. We really only master something after we have effectively taught it to someone else. Teaching is the final step of learning.

c. **You need someone to teach you again the first principles of the oracles of God**: This isn't to their credit. It isn't that **the first principles** are "beneath" the mature Christian. Rather, the sense is that one should be able to teach one's self, and remind one's self of these **first principles of the oracles of God**.

3. (12b-14) A contrast between *milk* and *solid food*.

And you have come to need milk and not solid food. For everyone who partakes *only* of milk *is* unskilled in the word of righteousness, for he is a babe. But solid food belongs to those who are of full age, *that is,* those who by reason of use have their senses exercised to discern both good and evil.

a. **And you have come to need milk**: **Milk** corresponds to the *first principles* of Hebrews 6:12. **Solid food** is the "meatier" material such as understanding the connection between Jesus and Melchizedek. It isn't that **milk** is bad; but these Christians should have added **solid food** to their diet. Peter reminds us all *as newborn babes, desire the pure milk of the word, that you may grow thereby* (1 Peter 2:2).

b. **For he is a babe**: In the ancient Greek, the sense of this phrase is *for he has become a babe* (Newell). There is nothing more delightful than a true babe in Jesus. But there is nothing more irritating and depressing than someone who *should* be mature but who has *become* **a babe**.

> i. Have you **become a babe**? Perhaps your Christian life is unstable. Babies are handed from one person to another, and spiritual babes are *tossed to and fro by every wind of doctrine* (Ephesians 4:14-16).

> ii. Have you **become a babe**? Perhaps you are divisive in your Christian life. Babies each have their own crib that they stick to, and spiritual babes have their particular denomination or church that they think of as "my church."

> iii. Have you **become a babe**? Perhaps you are star-struck by Christian celebrities of one kind or another. Babies are focused on one particular person (their mother), and spiritual babes glory in men (*I am of Paul, I am of Apollos*, as in 1 Corinthians 1:12).

> iv. Have you **become a babe**? Perhaps you are spiritually asleep. Babies need a lot of sleep, and spiritual babes spend much time spiritually asleep.

> v. Have you **become a babe**? Perhaps you are fussy and cranky with others. Babies can be cranky, and spiritual babes will fuss over any little thing.

c. **Is unskilled in the word of righteousness**: Those who have *become* babes reveal themselves because they are **unskilled in the word of righteousness**. We don't expect brand new Christians to be *skilled* **in the word of righteousness**, but those who have been Christians for a time should be.

d. **Who by reason of use have their senses exercised to discern both good and evil**: Our **senses** are **exercised** (trained by practice and habit) **to discern both good and evil** (primarily doctrinally, more than morally). Our **senses** become **exercised** when we *use* them (**by reason of use**). When we decide to **use** discernment, we mature.

> i. "We may sharpen our senses by use. When I was in the tea-trade, my sense of touch and taste and smell became acute to discern quite

minute differences. We need a similar acuteness in discerning good and evil." (Meyer)

ii. These Christians demonstrated immaturity by both their lack of discernment between **good and evil** and in their contemplation of giving up with Jesus. The mature Christian is marked by their discernment and by their unshakable commitment to Jesus Christ.

iii. Vincent on **good and evil**: "Not moral good and evil, but wholesome and corrupt doctrine. The implication is that the readers' condition is such as to prevent them from making this distinction."

iv. The ability to **discern** is a critical measure of spiritual maturity. Babies will put *anything* in their mouth. Spiritual babes are weak in discernment, and will accept any kind of spiritual food.

e. **Have their senses exercised**: It can be said that all five human senses have their spiritual counterparts.

i. We have a spiritual sense of taste: *If indeed you have tasted that the Lord is gracious* (1 Peter 2:3). *Taste and see that the LORD is good!* (Psalm 34:8)

ii. We have a spiritual sense of hearing: *Hear and your soul shall live* (Isaiah 55:3). *He who has an ear, let him hear what the Spirit says to the churches* (Revelation 2:7).

iii. We have a spiritual sense of sight: *Open my eyes, that I may see wondrous things from Your law* (Psalm 119:18). *The eyes of your understanding* (heart) *being enlightened* (Ephesians 1:18).

iv. We have a spiritual sense of smell: *He shall be of quick scent in the fear of the LORD* (Isaiah 11:3, RV margin). *I am full, having received from... you, a sweet-smelling aroma* (Philippians 4:18).

v. We have a spiritual sense of touch or feeling: *Because your heart was tender, and you humbled yourself before the LORD* (2 Kings 22:19). *The hardening of their heart; who being past feeling, have given themselves over to licentiousness* (Ephesians 4:18-19).

Hebrews 6 - A Warning to Discouraged Believers

A. The essential nature of maturity.

1. (1a) Going beyond the basics.

Therefore, leaving the discussion of the elementary *principles* of Christ, let us go on to perfection,

> a. **Therefore**: The writer rebuked his readers for their spiritual immaturity but he knew that nothing was gained by treating them as immature. He continued with his instruction and warnings.

> b. **Elementary principles**: This has the idea of "rudiments" or "ABCs." They are basic building blocks that are necessary, but must be built upon - otherwise has only a foundation and no structure.

> c. **Perfection**: This is the ancient Greek word *teleiotes*, which is much better understood as "maturity." The writer to the Hebrews did say that we can reach perfection on this side of eternity, but that we can and should reach a place of maturity in Jesus. The call is plain: **let us go on to perfection**.

> > i. "*Teleiotes* does not imply complete knowledge but a certain maturity in the Christian faith." (Barclay)

2. (1b-2) Some of the "basics" to go beyond.

Not laying again the foundation of repentance from dead works and of faith toward God, of the doctrine of baptisms, of laying on of hands, of resurrection of the dead, and of eternal judgment.

> a. **Not laying again the foundation**: These *elementary principles* are given in three pairs. **Repentance** and **faith** go together. **Baptisms** and **laying on of hands** go together. **Resurrection of the dead** and **eternal judgment** are paired together.

> b. **Not laying again the foundation**: Many people regard this as a Biblical list of important elementary principles for the Christian life. Bible study

and discipleship series have been taught developing each one of these topics, with the thought that this is a good list of basic doctrines. But that wasn't the writer's point here at all.

    i. To understand this list, one must ask basic questions:

- What is distinctively *Christian* about this list?
- Where is the specific mention of Jesus or salvation by grace alone?
- Could one believe in or practice these things and still not be a follower of Jesus Christ, and not believe Him to be the Messiah?

    ii. "When we consider the 'rudiments' one by one, it is remarkable how little in the list is distinctive of Christianity, for practically every item could have its place in a fairly orthodox Jewish community... Each of them, indeed, acquires a new significance in a Christian context; but the impression we get is that existing Jewish beliefs and practices were used as a foundation on which to build Christian truth." (Bruce)

    iii. "It is profoundly significant to observe how little distinctively Christian there is in this statement. Repentance, faith, resurrection, and judgment were certainly Jewish, and on this account the reference seems to be the Jewish foundation, and they are urged to avoid these elementary things which they are to leave for something higher and richer." (Griffith Thomas)

c. **Of the doctrine of baptisms**: Not even **baptisms**, as it is used in this passage, is necessarily Christian. The specific ancient Greek word here translated **baptisms** (*baptismos*) is *not* the word regularly used in the New Testament to describe Christian baptism (*baptizo*). *Baptismos* is the word used on three other specific instances to refer to Jewish ceremonial washings (Hebrews 9:10, Mark 7:4, and Mark 7:8).

    i. The New English Bible translation reflects this, translating "**doctrine of baptisms**" as *instruction about cleansing rites*. The ESV translation has, *instruction about washings*.

    ii. Bruce quotes Nairne: "'Doctrines of washings'--how unnatural are the attempts to explain this plural as referring to Christian Baptism."

d. **The foundation**: In this case, the *elementary principles* to move beyond are all items in a common ground of belief between Christianity and Judaism. This was a safe common ground for these discouraged Jewish Christians to retreat back to.

    i. Because Christianity did grow out of Judaism, it was a more subtle temptation for a Jewish Christian to slip back into Judaism than it was for a formerly pagan Christian to go back to his pagan ways. "Part of the problem facing the Hebrews was the superficial similarity between the elementary tenets of Christianity and those of Judaism, which made it possible for Christian Jews to think they could hold on to both." (Guthrie)

ii. Of course, these Jewish Christians did not want to abandon *religion*, but they did want to make it less distinctively *Christian*. Therefore, they went back to this common ground to avoid persecution. Living in this comfortable common ground, one did not stick out so much. A Jew and a Christian together could say, "Let's repent, let's have faith, let's perform ceremonial washings," and so forth. This was a subtle yet certain denial of Jesus.

iii. This is entirely characteristic of those who feel discouraged, and wish to give up. There is always the temptation to still be religious, but not so fanatical about Jesus.

3. (3) A statement of hope and dependence on God.

And this we will do if God permits.

a. **If God permits**: This should not be taken as implying that God may not want them to go on to maturity, past those basics common to Christianity and Judaism.

b. **If God permits**: Instead, this expresses the believers' complete dependence on God. If we do press on to maturity, we realize that it only happens at God's pleasure.

B. The danger of falling away.

Preface: Understanding an approach to controversial passages like this.

a. There is a great temptation to shape a difficult passage in to what we *think* it *should* say, according to our theology system or bent. Yet we must first be concerned with understanding what the text says (exposition), before we are concerned with fitting what it says into a system of theology.

b. Systems of theology have some value, as they show how Biblical ideas are connected and show that the Bible *does not* contradict itself. But the way to right systems *begins with a right understanding of the text, not one that bends the text to fit into a system.*

i. "We come to this passage ourselves with the intention to read it with the simplicity of a child, and whatever we find therein to state it; and if it may not seem to agree with something we have hitherto held, we are prepared to cast away every doctrine of our own, rather than one passage of Scripture." (Spurgeon)

ii. "We had better far be inconsistent with ourselves than with the inspired Word. I have been called an Arminian Calvinist or a Calvinistic Arminian, and I am quite content so long as I can keep close to my Bible." (Spurgeon)

c. Satan knows Scripture, and this passage has rightly been called "one of the Devil's favorite passages" for the way it can (out of context) condemn the struggling believer. Many Christians feel like giving up after hearing Satan "preach a sermon" on this text.

1. (4-6) The impossibility of repentance for those who fall away after receiving blessing from God.

For *it is* impossible for those who were once enlightened, and have tasted the heavenly gift, and have become partakers of the Holy Spirit, and have tasted the good word of God and the powers of the age to come, if they fall away, to renew them again to repentance, since they crucify again for themselves the Son of God, and put *Him* to an open shame.

a. **For it is impossible**: The word **impossible** is put in a position of emphasis. The writer to the Hebrews does not say this is merely difficult, but that it is without possibility.

  i. Note the other uses of **impossible** in Hebrews:

  • It is *impossible* for God to lie (Hebrews 6:18).

  • It is *impossible* that the blood of bulls and goats can take away sin (Hebrews 10:4).

  • It is *impossible* to please God without faith (Hebrews 11:6).

  ii. "This word **impossible** *stands immovable*." (Alford)

b. **Who were once enlightened, and have tasted the heavenly gift, and have become partakers of the Holy Spirit, and have tasted the good word of God and the powers of the age to come**: The writer to the Hebrews speaks of people with impressive spiritual experiences. The big debate is whether this is the experience of *salvation* or the experience of something *short of salvation*. Looking at each descriptive word helps see what kind of experience this describes.

  i. **Enlightened**: This ancient Greek word has the same meaning as the English word. It described the experience of light shining on someone, of a "new light" shining on the mind and spirit.

  ii. **Tasted**: The idea of "tasting" *may* mean to "test" something. But other uses of this word indicate a full, real experience as in how Jesus *tasted death* in Hebrews 2:9. **The heavenly gift** is probably salvation (as in Romans 6:23 and Ephesians 2:8).

iii. **Partakers of the Holy Spirit**: This is an unique term in the New Testament. Since it means "sharing" the Holy Spirit, it has to do with receiving and having fellowship with the Holy Spirit.

iv. **Tasted the good word of God**: This means they experienced the goodness of God's word, and saw its goodness at work in them.

v. **The powers of the age of come**: This is a way to describe God's supernatural power. The writer to the Hebrews describes those who experienced God's supernatural power.

c. **If they fall away, to renew them again to repentance**: One of the most heated debates over any New Testament passage is focused on this text. The question is simple: Are these people with these impressive spiritual experiences in fact Christians? Are they God's elect, chosen before the foundation of the world?

i. Commentators divide on this issue, usually deciding the issue with great certainty but with no agreement.

ii. One the one side we see clearly that someone can have great spiritual experiences and still not be saved (Matthew 7:21-23). One can even do many religious things and still not be saved. The Pharisees of New Testament times are a good example of this principle. These men did many religious things but were not saved or submitted to God. These ancient Pharisees:

- Energetically evangelized (Matthew 23:15).
- Impressively prayed (Matthew 23:14).
- Made rigorous religious commitments (Matthew 23:16).
- Strictly and carefully tithed (Matthew 23:23).
- Honored religious traditions (Matthew 23:29-31).
- Practiced fasting regularly (Luke 18:12).
- Yet Jesus called them *sons of Hell* (Matthew 23:15).

iii. Yet, from a *human perspective*, it is doubtful that anyone who seemed to have the credentials mentioned in Hebrews 6:4-5 would *not* be regarded a true Christian. God knows their ultimate destiny and hopefully the individual does also - yet from all outward appearance, such Christian experience might qualify a man to be an elder in many churches. Yet beyond the knowledge hidden in the mind of God and the individual in question, from all *human observation*, we must say these are Christians spoken of in Hebrews 6:4-5. A good example of this is Demas.

- Paul warmly greeted other Christians on his behalf (Colossians 4:14).

- Demas is called a *fellow worker* with Paul (Philemon 24).

- Yet Paul condemned Demas, at least hinting at apostasy (2 Timothy 4:10).

iv. Taking all this together, we see that it is possible to display some fruit or spiritual growth - then to die spiritually, showing that the "soil of the heart" was never right (Mark 4:16-19).

v. Therefore, eternal standing of those written of in Hebrews 6:4-6 is a question with two answers. We may safely say that from a human perspective, they had all appearance of salvation. Nevertheless, from the perspective of God's perfect wisdom it is impossible to say on this side of eternity.

d. **For it is impossible... if they fall away, to renew them again to repentance**: Despite their impressive spiritual experience - or at least the appearance of it - these are in grave danger. **If they fall away**, it is **impossible** for them to repent.

i. If these are genuine Christians who "lost their salvation," the terrible fact is that they can *never* regain it. In the early church some groups (such as the Montanists and the Novatianists) used this passage to teach there was *no possibility* of restoration if someone sinned significantly after their baptism.

ii. Others explain it by saying that this is all merely a hypothetical warning (in light of the statement in Hebrews 6:9). In this thinking, the writer to the Hebrews never intended to say that his readers were really in danger of damnation. He only used a *hypothetical* danger to motivate them. However, one must say that there is questionable value in warning someone against something that can't happen.

iii. Still others think that this penalty deals only with reward, not with salvation itself. They stress the idea that it says **repentance** is **impossible**, not *salvation*. Therefore these are Christians of low commitment and experience who risk a loss of all heavenly reward, saved only "by the skin of their teeth."

iv. This difficult passage is best understood in the *context* of Hebrews 6:1-2. The writer to the Hebrews means that if they retreat back to Judaism, all the religious "repentance" in the world will do them no good. Retreating from distinctive Christianity into the "safe" ideas and customs of their former religious experience is to forsake Jesus, and to essentially crucify Him again. This is especially true for these ancient

Christians from a Jewish background, since the religious customs they took up again likely included animal sacrifice for atonement, denying the total work of Jesus for them on the cross.

e. **If they fall away**: There is a necessary distinction between *falling* and *falling* **away**. Falling away is more than falling into sin; it is actually departing from Jesus Himself. *For a righteous man may fall seven times and rise again, but the wicked shall fall by calamity* (Proverbs 24:16). The difference is between a Peter and a Judas. If you depart from Jesus (**fall away**) there is no hope.

i. The message to these Christians who felt like giving up was clear: if you don't continue on with Jesus, don't suppose you will find salvation by just going on with the ideas and experience that Christianity and Judaism share. If you aren't saved in Jesus, you aren't saved at all. There is no salvation in a safe "common ground" that is not distinctively *Christian*.

ii. If someone falls away we must understand *why* he or she can't repent - it is because *they don't want to*. It is not as if God *prohibits* their repentance. Since repentance itself is a work of God (Romans 2:4), the desire to repent is evidence that he or she has not truly fallen away.

iii. The idea is not that "if you fall away, you can't ever come back to Jesus." Instead, the idea is "if you turn your back on Jesus, don't expect to find salvation anywhere else, especially in the practice of religion apart from the fullness of Jesus."

iv. "This passage has nothing to do with those who fear lest it condemns them. The presence of that anxiety, like the cry which betrayed the real mother in the days of Solomon, establishes beyond a doubt that you are not one that has fallen away beyond the possibility of renewal to repentance." (Meyer)

2. (7-8) An illustration of the serious consequences of falling away.

For the earth which drinks in the rain that often comes upon it, and bears herbs useful for those by whom it is cultivated, receives blessing from God; but if it bears thorns and briars, *it is* rejected and near to being cursed, whose end *is* to be burned.

a. **For the earth which drinks in the rain... and bears herbs useful... receives blessing from God**: When the **earth** receives rain and **bears** useful plants, it fulfills its purpose and justifies the blessing of rain sent upon it. The writer to the Hebrews applies the point: "You've been blessed. But where is the fruit?" God looks for what grows in us after He blesses us, especially looking for what grows in terms of maturity.

b. **But if it bears thorns and briars, it is rejected**: If ground is blessed by rain but refuses to bear fruit, no one blames the farmer for burning it. The idea shows that growth and bearing fruit are important to keep from falling away. When we really bear fruit, we abide in Jesus (John 15:5) and are in no danger of falling away.

C. Don't be discouraged.

1. (9) The writer admits he is a little more harsh than he needs to be.

But, beloved, we are confident of better things concerning you, yes, things that accompany salvation, though we speak in this manner.

a. **We are confident of better things concerning you**: Though he spoke so severely, the writer to the Hebrews was confident His readers would continue on with Jesus. He thinks of their continuation in the faith as one of the **things that accompany salvation**.

b. **Though we speak in this manner**: These encouraging words after the strong warning of Hebrews 6:4-8 should not be understood to mean that the warnings in the previous verses are not serious, or that the writer warned of impossible consequences. If anything, verse nine shows how badly these struggling Christians needed *encouragement*. Their spiritual danger was not so much out of a calculated rebellion, but more because of a depressing discouragement. They need warning, but also needed encouragement.

2. (10-12) Don't be discouraged because God hasn't forgotten about you.

For God *is* not unjust to forget your work and labor of love which you have shown toward His name, *in that* you have ministered to the saints, and do minister. And we desire that each one of you show the same diligence to the full assurance of hope until the end, that you do not become sluggish, but imitate those who through faith and patience inherit the promises.

a. **God is not unjust to forget your work and labor of love**: When we are discouraged we sometimes think God forgets us and all we have done for Him and for His people. But God would deny His own nature if He forgot such things (He would be **unjust**). God sees and remembers.

i. Sometimes our fear that God forgot our **work and labor of love** comes from relying on the attention and applause of people. It is true that some *people* may **forget your work and labor of love**, but God never will.

b. **We desire that each one of you show the same diligence to the full assurance of hope until the end**: The writer to the Hebrews encouraged like a coach, urging believers to press on. The followers of Jesus must keep up their good **work**; press on with that hope **until the end**; and imitate those who **inherit** (not earn) God's promises. When we fail to do this, discouragement often makes us **become sluggish**.

c. **But imitate those who through faith and patience inherit the promises**: Instead of giving in to discouragement, imitate those who found the key to gaining God's promises - **faith and patience**, as demonstrated by Abraham.

> i. We are grateful to remember Abraham's life and to see that he did not have a *perfect* faith or a *perfect* patience. If Abraham had some of our weakness then we can have some of his **faith and patience**.

d. **Do not become sluggish**: The idea is that we should not let discouragement make us **sluggish**, leading to the sense that we may as well give up. First we lose the desire to *press* on; then we lose the desire to *go* on.

> i. Before he was king, David showed a great answer to discouragement: *David encouraged himself in the Lord his God* (1 Samuel 30:6, KJV). It is a blessing when others encourage us, but we don't have to wait for that. We can encourage our self in the Lord.

3. (13-18) Don't be discouraged, because God's promises are reliable.

For when God made a promise to Abraham, because He could swear by no one greater, He swore by Himself, saying, "Surely blessing I will bless you, and multiplying I will multiply you." And so, after he had patiently endured, he obtained the promise. For men indeed swear by the greater, and an oath for confirmation *is* for them an end of all dispute. Thus God, determining to show more abundantly to the heirs of promise the immutability of His counsel, confirmed *it* by an oath, that by two immutable things, in which it *is* impossible for God to lie, we might have strong consolation, who have fled for refuge to lay hold of the hope set before *us*.

a. **After he had patiently endured**: A season of patient endurance is a time of spiritual attack. It seems that we may never obtain **the promise** of God in our life. It is easy to wonder, "Will God *really* come through in my situation?"

b. **After he had patiently endured, he obtained the promise**: God came through for Abraham, even sealing His **promise** with an oath. In fact, **because He could swear by no one greater, He swore by Himself**. This oath showed that God's promises (like His character) are unchanging. Abraham's trust in this was the gateway to the fulfillment of the promise.

> i. "This passage teaches us...that an oath may be lawfully used by Christians; and this ought to be particularly observed, on account of

fanatical men who are disposed to abrogate the practices of solemn swearing which God has prescribed in his Law." (Calvin)

c. **That by two immutable things, in which it is impossible for God to lie, we might have strong consolation**: The **two immutable** (unchanging) **things** are God's *promise* and God's *oath*. It is **impossible for God to lie** in either of these two things.

> i. The *absolute reliability* of God's promise should impress us. "Now, brethren, who among us dare doubt this? Where is the hardy sinner who dares come forward and say, 'I impugn the oath of God'? Oh! But let us blush the deepest scarlet, and scarlet is but white compared with the blush which ought to mantle the cheek of every child of God to think that even God's own children should, in effect, accuse their heavenly Father of perjury. Oh, shame upon us!" (Spurgeon)

d. **Strong consolation**: God isn't content to give us mere **consolation**. He wants to give us **strong consolation**. Spurgeon described some characteristics of strong consolation:

- Strong consolation does not depend upon bodily health.

- Strong consolation does not depend upon the excitement of public services and Christian fellowship.

- Strong consolation can't be shaken by human reasoning.

- Strong consolation is stronger than our guilty conscience.

> i. "It is a strong consolation that can deal with outward trials when a man has poverty staring him in the face, and hears his little children crying for bread; when bankruptcy is likely to come upon him through unavoidable losses; when the poor man has just lost his wife, and his dear children have been put into the same grave; when one after another all earthly props and comforts have given way, it needs a strong consolation then; not in your pictured trials, but your real trials, not in your imaginary whimsied afflictions, but in the real afflictions, and the blustering storms of life. To rejoice then, and say, 'Though these things be not with me as I would have them, yet hath he made with me an everlasting covenant ordered in all things and sure;' this is strong consolation." (Spurgeon)

e. **Who have fled for refuge to lay hold of the hope set before us**: This is another reason for encouragement, knowing that God has a **refuge** of **hope set before us**. We can think of this **refuge** of **hope** are like the cities of refuge commanded by the Law of Moses, as described in Numbers 35.

- Both Jesus and the cities of refuge are *within easy reach* of the person in need. The place of refuge is of no use if it can't be reached.

- Both Jesus and the cities of refuge are *open to all*, not just the Israelite. No one who comes the place of refuge is turned away in time of need.

- Both Jesus and the cities of refuge were *places to live*. In time of need, one never came to a city of refuge just to look around.

- Both Jesus and the cities of refuge are the *only alternative* for the one in need. Without this refuge destruction is certain.

- Both Jesus and the cities of refuge provide protection *only within their boundaries*. To go outside the provided refuge means death.

- Both Jesus and the cities of refuge provided full freedom with the *death of the High Priest.*

- However, there is *a crucial distinction* between Jesus and the cities of refuge. The cities of refuge only helped the *innocent*; the *guilty* can come to Jesus and find refuge.

4. (19-20) Don't be discouraged, because Jesus will lead us into God's glory.

This *hope* we have as an anchor of the soul, both sure and steadfast, and which enters the Presence *behind* the veil, where the forerunner has entered for us, *even* Jesus, having become High Priest forever according to the order of Melchizedek.

a. **This hope we have as an anchor**: The **anchor** was a common figure for **hope** in the ancient world. Here the idea is that we are anchored to something firm but unseen (**which enters the Presence behind the veil**).

i. You don't need an **anchor** for calm seas. The rougher the weather, the more important your **anchor** is.

- We need the anchor to hold the ship and keep it from being wrecked.

- We need the anchor to stabilize the ship and keep it more comfortable for those on board.

- We need the anchor to allow the ship to maintain the progress it has made.

ii. The ship must have hold of the anchor, even as we must lay hold of hope. The anchor itself may have a strong grip, and be secured to the ocean floor, yet if it isn't securely attached to the ship it is of no use. But there is also a sense in which the anchor has hold of the ship, even as hope has hold of us.

iii. But the **anchor** analogy doesn't apply perfectly. We are anchored *upward in heaven*, not down in the ground; and we are anchored to *move on*, not to stand still.

iv. "Our anchor is like every other, when it is of any use it is out of sight. When a man sees the anchor it is doing nothing, unless it happen to be some small stream anchor or grapnel in shallow water. When the anchor is of use it is gone: there it went overboard with a splash; far down there, all among the fish, lies the iron holdfast, quite out of sight. Where is your hope, brother? Do you believe because you can see? That is not believing at all." (Spurgeon)

b. **Which enters the Presence behind the veil, where the forerunner has entered for us**: This confident, anchor-like hope sees us into the very **presence** of God. **Hope** is exactly the medicine discouraged Christians need.

c. **The forerunner...even Jesus**: We are assured of this access into the presence of God because Jesus has entered as a **forerunner**. The Old Testament high priest did not enter the veil as a *forerunner*, only as a *representative*. But Jesus has entered into the immediate **presence** of God the Father so that His people can follow Him there.

i. A **forerunner** (the ancient Greek word *prodromos*) was a military reconnaissance man. A **forerunner** goes forward, knowing that others will follow behind him.

ii. "We are told next that as a fore-runner our Lord has *for us* entered - that is entered to take possession in our name. When Jesus Christ went into heaven he did as it were look around on all the thrones, and all the palms, and all the harps, and all the crowns, and say 'I take possession of all these in the name of my redeemed. I am their representative and claim the heavenly places in their name.'" (Spurgeon)

iii. Yet if Jesus is the forerunner, we are then the *after-runners*. There is no forerunner if there are no after-runners. We should follow hard after Jesus, and run hard after Him. He has gone before us and He is our pattern.

d. **Behind the veil... having become High Priest forever according to the order of Melchizedek**: The temple analogy (**behind the veil**) reminds the writer to the Hebrews of his previous start into the subject of Jesus as our **High Priest forever according to the order of Melchizedek** (in Hebrews 5:6-10). This thought continues into the next chapter.

Hebrews 7 - A Better Priesthood, a Better High Priest

A. The theme of Hebrews 7.

1. The writer to the Hebrews now explains a theme that he introduced back in Hebrews 2:17: Jesus as our High Priest.

a. He began to discuss the issue in Hebrews 5:10, but had to spend some time warning these discouraged Christians about the danger of not continuing and progressing in their Christian life.

b. Like the writer of a good detective story, the writer to the Hebrews draws out a character from the Old Testament that many might think insignificant, and he brings that character into real prominence.

2. These Christians from a Jewish background were interested in Jesus as their High Priest, but had a significant intellectual objection to the idea. This is because Jesus did not come from the priestly tribe (the tribe of Levi) or the priestly family in that tribe (the family of Aaron).

a. The writer to the Hebrews wanted to remove these intellectual problems the Jewish Christians had with the gospel. These intellectual hang-ups kept them from continuing on to maturity in Jesus.

b. In the same way, many Christians are hung up on intellectual issues that *could* be resolved, allowing them to move on with Jesus. If a Christian is hung up on issues like creation and evolution, the validity of miracles, or other such things, they should get the issues resolved so they can move on with Jesus.

3. This chapter is also important because it shows us how we should think of the Old Testament institutions of the priesthood and the Law.

B. Melchizedek and his relation to the Aaronic priesthood.

1. (1-3) What we know of Melchizedek from Genesis 14:18-20.

For this Melchizedek, king of Salem, priest of the Most High God, who met Abraham returning from the slaughter of the kings and blessed him, to whom also Abraham gave a tenth part of all, first being translated "king of righteousness," and then also king of Salem, meaning "king of peace," without father, without mother, without genealogy, having neither beginning of days nor end of life, but made like the Son of God, remains a priest continually.

a. **Who met Abraham returning from the slaughter of the kings**: After Abraham defeated the confederation of kings who took his nephew Lot captive, he met with a mysterious **priest** named **Melchizedek**, who was also **king** over the city **of Salem** (an ancient name for the city of Jeru*salem*).

i. History shows the danger of combining religious and civic authority. Therefore God did not allow the kings of Israel to be priests and the priests to be kings. **Melchizedek**, who was the **king of Salem** and **priest of the Most High God** was an unique exception.

b. **Priest of the Most High God**: Melchizedek was not merely a worshipper of the true God. He had the honored title **priest of the Most High God**. The greatness of God magnified the greatness of Melchizedek's priesthood.

i. "Any priesthood is evaluated according to the status of the deity who is served, which means that Melchizedek's must have been of a highly exalted kind." (Guthrie)

c. **And blessed him**: Melchizedek blessed Abraham, and Abraham gave Melchizedek a tithe, which is **a tenth part of all** (all the spoils of battle, as mentioned in Genesis 14:20).

d. **First being translated "king of righteousness," and then also king of Salem, meaning "king of peace"**: The name **Melchizedek** means **"king of righteousness,"** and he was also **"king of peace"** (because the name **Salem** means "**peace**").

i. The order is subtle but important. First, Melchizedek in his very name was called **"king of righteousness."** *Then* he was called **"king of peace."** As always, **righteousness** comes before **peace**. Righteousness is the only true path to peace. People look for that peace in *escape*, in *evasion*, or in *compromise*, but they will only find it in righteousness. "Peace without righteousness is like the smooth surface of the stream ere it takes its awful Niagara plunge." (Spurgeon)

ii. The fact that these names have meaning, and that the Holy Spirit explains the meaning shows that each word is important and inspired by God. "A teaching was intended by the Holy Spirit in the names: so the apostle instructs us in the passage before us. I believe in the verbal inspiration of Scripture; hence, I can see how there can be instruction for us even in the proper names of persons and of places. Those who reject verbal inspiration must in effect condemn the great apostle of the Gentiles, whose teaching is so frequently based upon a word. He makes more of words and names than any of us should have thought of doing, and he was guided therein by the Spirit of the Lord, and therefore he was right. For my part, I am far mores afraid of making too little of the Word than of seeing too much in it." (Spurgeon)

e. **Without father, without mother**: There is nothing said about the genealogy of Melchizedek in the Genesis 14 passage or anywhere else. As far as the Biblical record is concerned, he has no **father** or **mother**, no **beginning of days nor end of life**. "We see but little of him, yet we see nothing little in him." (Spurgeon)

i. Though virtually all the commentators disagree with each other on this point, some think that **without father, without mother, without genealogy, having neither beginning of days nor end of life, but made like the Son of God** means that Melchizedek was a heavenly being, if not a pre-incarnate appearance of Jesus Himself.

f. **Made like the Son of God**: Melchizedek was **made like the Son of God**. It really isn't that Jesus has Melchizedek's kind of priesthood. Instead, Melchizedek has *Jesus'* kind of priesthood.

i. **Made like** in Hebrews 7:3 translates the ancient Greek word *aphomoiomenos*, a word used nowhere else in the New Testament. "It is a suggestive word, used in the active of 'a facsimile copy or model' and in the passive of 'being made similar to'." (Guthrie)

ii. "It was as if the Father could not await the day of His Son's priestly entrance within the veil; but must needs anticipate the marvels of His ministry, by embodying its leading features in miniature." (Meyer)

g. **Remains a priest continually**: Either this refers to the continuation of the priestly order of Melchizedek, or it is evidence that Melchizedek was actually Jesus appearing in the Old Testament. Jesus' priesthood does remain to this day, and into eternity.

2. (4-10) Melchizedek is greater than Abraham because Abraham paid tithes to Melchizedek, and because Melchizedek blessed Abraham.

Now consider how great this man *was*, to whom even the patriarch Abraham gave a tenth of the spoils. And indeed those who are of the sons of Levi, who receive the priesthood, have a commandment to receive tithes from the people according to the law, that is, from their brethren, though they have come from the loins of Abraham; but he

whose genealogy is not derived from them received tithes from Abraham and blessed him who had the promises. Now beyond all contradiction the lesser is blessed by the better. Here mortal men receive tithes, but there he *receives them*, of whom it is witnessed that he lives. Even Levi, who receives tithes, paid tithes through Abraham, so to speak, for he was still in the loins of his father when Melchizedek met him.

a. **Abraham gave a tenth of the spoils... the sons of Levi... have a commandment to receive tithes from the people according to the law**: The priesthood of Levi received tithes from Israel as a **commandment**. Abraham *voluntarily* gave tithes to Melchizedek. This makes Abraham's *giving* to Melchizedek greater than Israel's *payment* of tithes to the priesthood instituted by Moses.

i. **A tenth of the spoils**: **Spoils** is literally *the top of the heap*, referring to the choicest spoils of war. When Abraham tithed to Melchizedek he literally "took it off the top."

b. **Even Levi, who receives tithes, paid tithes through Abraham, so to speak, for he was still in the loins of his father when Melchizedek met him**: Because the whole tribe of Levi was genetically **in the loins of** Abraham when he did this, we see the Old Testament priesthood paying tithes to the priesthood of Melchizedek. This shows Melchizedek is in a position of authority over Abraham and his descendant Levi.

i. The phrase, "**so to speak**" in Hebrews 7:9 is important. The writer to the Hebrews knows he is making an allegorical point, so he doesn't want to be taken *too* literally.

c. **The lesser is blessed by the greater**: This principle also shows that Melchizedek was **greater** than Abraham because he **blessed** Abraham. On his part, Abraham accepted that Melchizedek was **greater** when he received the blessing.

i. "The blessing here spoken of... is not the simple *wishing of good* to others, which may be done by inferiors to superiors; but it is the action of a person *authorized* to declare *God's intention* to bestow good things on another." (Macknight, cited by Clarke)

C. The need for a new priesthood.

1. (11) The Levitical priesthood never made anything perfect.

Therefore, if perfection were through the Levitical priesthood (for under it the people received the law), what further need *was there* that another priest should rise according to the order of Melchizedek, and not be called according to the order of Aaron?

a. **If perfection were through the Levitical priesthood**: This shows the *need* for a different order of priesthood. If **perfection** could come **through the Levitical priesthood**, there would be no need for another priesthood. Yet God described another priesthood in Psalm 110:4.

i. The simple fact that God describes a **priest... according to the order of Melchizedek** in Psalm 110:4 shows there is something lacking in the priesthood **according to the order of Aaron**. God would never establish an unnecessary priesthood.

ii. The term **Levitical priesthood** simply describes the Jewish priesthood of the Old Testament. It is called **Levitical** because most of the instructions for the Old Testament priesthood are found in the Book of Leviticus.

b. **Under it the people received the law**: The Old Testament priesthood is the priesthood associated with the Law of Moses. The priesthood of Melchizedek is associated with Abraham, not with Moses.

2. (12) The changing priesthood and the change of the place of Moses' Law.

For the priesthood being changed, of necessity there is also a change of the law.

a. **The priesthood being changed**: This is logically developed from Psalm 110:4. God would never introduce a new priesthood if it was not necessary, and He would never introduce an inferior priesthood. The mere mention of *the order of Melchizedek* (in Psalm 110:4 and Hebrews 7:11) shows that God wanted the priesthood to be **changed**.

b. **Of necessity**: The priesthood of Aaron was connected to the Law of Moses. So if the priesthood is changed we should also anticipate some change of the Law's status or place.

3. (13-14) Jesus could not be a priest according to the Mosaic Law because He is from the wrong tribe.

For He of whom these things are spoken belongs to another tribe, from which no man has officiated at the altar. For *it is* evident that our Lord arose from Judah, of which tribe Moses spoke nothing concerning priesthood.

a. **Another tribe, from which no man has officiated at the altar**: Under the Law of Moses, God strictly commanded that only those from the family of Aaron could serve **at the altar** in sacrifice.

b. **He of whom these things are spoken belongs to another tribe**: Jesus is obviously not from the family of Aaron or even the tribe of Levi. The tribe of **Judah** (the tribe of Jesus' lineage) had nothing to do with Aaron's priesthood, the priesthood associated with the Law of Moses. Therefore according to the priesthood of Aaron and the Law of Moses, Jesus could never be a priest. If He is our High Priest, it must be under another principle.

4. (15-17) God's declaration that the Messiah belongs to another order of priesthood in Psalm 110:4.

And it is yet far more evident if, in the likeness of Melchizedek, there arises another priest who has come, not according to the law of a fleshly commandment, but according to the power of an endless life. For He testifies:

"You *are* a priest forever
According to the order of Melchizedek."

a. **Not according to the law of a fleshly commandment**: Jesus' priesthood is not based upon law or heredity (**a fleshly commandment**), but upon the power of God's **endless life**.

b. **You are a priest *forever***: This could be said of the Messiah, who was a priest according to the order of Melchizedek. It could never be said of a priest according to the order of Aaron, none of who had **the power of an endless life** and each of who served a limited term as priests - limited to their own life span.

c. **According to the power of an endless life**: Matthew 27:1 says, *When morning came, all the chief priests and elders of the people plotted against Jesus to put Him to death.* Among those who conspired to put Jesus to death, there were priests of the order of Aaron. But by the **power of an endless life** Jesus showed that His priesthood was superior when He triumphed over death.

5. (18-19) Why the law is set aside as the way of establishing our relationship and access to God.

For on the one hand there is an annulling of the former commandment because of its weakness and unprofitableness, for the law made nothing perfect; on the other hand, *there is the* bringing in of a better hope, through which we draw near to God.

a. **Because of its weakness and unprofitableness**: In its **weakness** and **unprofitableness**, the law **made nothing perfect**. The law does a great job of setting God's perfect standard but it does not give the power to keep that standard.

i. "Let all legalists mark this: **The Law made nothing perfect**. Let the Seventh Day Adventists mark: **The Law made nothing perfect**. Let all those who dream of the Law as a rule of life remember: **The Law made nothing perfect**." (Newell)

b. **The law made nothing perfect**: Therefore, the law is valuable as it shows us God's perfect standard, but it was not ultimately intended to be the basis of a man's walk with God. This is because the law is *weak* and *unprofitable* when it comes to saving my soul or giving me power over sin.

i. The law provides expert diagnosis of our sin problem, which is absolutely essential. But the law does not provide the cure to our sin problem. Only Jesus can save us from our sin problem.

c. **On the other hand**: Since now, in Jesus, we have a **better hope, through which we draw near to God**, we are wrong to go back to building our Christian walk on the law. Therefore the law is "annulled" or set aside in the sense that it no longer is the dominating principle of our life, especially of our relationship with God.

i. "The Greek word translated disannuling [**annulling**], *athetesis*, is the same as appears in Hebrews 9:26 for the *putting away of sin* 'by the sacrifice of Himself.' *The disappearance of the Law is as absolute, therefore, as the putting away of sin!*" (Newell)

ii. The law does not give you a **better hope**. The law does not **draw** you **near** to God the way God's grace given in Jesus does. Yet many Christians live a legal relationship with God instead of a grace relationship with Him.

iii. "Although the law performed a valuable function, its essential *weakness* was that it could not give life and vitality even to those who kept it, let alone to those who did not. In fact its function was not to provide strength, but to provide a standard by which man could measure his own moral status. Its *uselessness* must not be regarded in the sense of being totally worthless, but in the sense of being ineffective in providing a constant means of approach to God based on a totally adequate sacrifice." (Guthrie)

d. **Annulling of the former commandment... bringing in of a better hope**: The writer came to the same conclusion about the law as Paul did in Galatians 3:19-25, but he got there in a totally different way. In Galatians, Paul showed the law as a tutor that brings us to Jesus. In Hebrews the law is associated with a priesthood that was been made obsolete by a superior priesthood.

i. "Cease to think of cleansing, and consider the Cleanser; forbear to speculate on deliverance, and deal with the Deliverer." (Meyer)

e. **A better hope, through which we draw near to God**: Because we have a better priesthood and a better High Priest, we also have a **better hope** and **draw near to God**. Our hope is in Jesus, not in the Law of Moses or our ability to keep it.

i. This should temper our excitement about the rebuilding of the temple in Jerusalem. The small cadres of dedicated Jews absolutely committed to rebuilding the temple have an exciting place in God's prophetic plan. But anyone who restores the Aaronic priesthood and resumes Levitical sacrifice (especially for atonement of sin) denies the superior priesthood and ultimate sacrifice of Jesus.

D. The superiority of our High Priest.

1. (20-21) Jesus was made High Priest by the direct oath of God.

And inasmuch as *He was* not *made priest* without an oath (for they have become priests without an oath, but He with an oath by Him who said to Him:

**"The LORD has sworn
And will not relent,
'You *are* a priest forever
According to the order of Melchizedek'"),**

a. **He was not made priest without an oath**: The priesthood of Jesus was established with an oath. It is recorded in Psalm 110:4: *The LORD has sworn and will not relent, "You are a priest forever According to the order of Melchizedek."*

b. **They have become priests without an oath**: The high priest of the order of Aaron was appointed by heredity, not by personal character or an oath of God. Not so with Jesus and the priestly **order of Melchizedek**. God even sealed His choice by an **oath**.

2. (22) Jesus: our guarantee of a better covenant.

By so much more Jesus has become a surety of a better covenant.

a. **Jesus has become a surety**: The ancient Greek word translated **surety** (*egguos*) described someone who gave security, who cosigned a loan to guarantee payment, or put up bail for a prisoner. **Jesus** *Himself* is the guarantee of **a better covenant**.

b. **A better covenant**: The Old Covenant had a mediator (Moses), but no one to guarantee the people's side of the covenant. Therefore they continually failed under it. But the New Covenant - **a better covenant** - has a cosigner to guarantee it on our behalf. Therefore, the New Covenant depends on what Jesus did, not on what we do. *He* is the **surety** and *we* are not.

c. **Covenant**: The word used for **covenant** (the ancient Greek word *diatheke*) is not the usual term for "covenant" (*syntheke*). The literal meaning of *diatheke* is closer to the idea of a "testament" in the sense of a "last will and testament." Perhaps the writer is trying to stress that while a covenant might be thought of as an agreement that two equal parties arrive at, the testator *dictates* a testament. The "agreement" under which we meet with God through Jesus is not something we have *negotiated* with Him. He has *dictated* the terms to us, and we will accept or reject the terms.

d. **By so much more**: This **much more** - the overwhelming superiority of Jesus Christ - proves He is worthy and able to be our guarantee, our cosigner of **a better covenant**.

3. (23-25) An unchanging priesthood means a lasting salvation.

Also there were many priests, because they were prevented by death from continuing. But He, because He continues forever, has an unchangeable priesthood. Therefore He is also able to save to the uttermost those who come to God through Him, since He always lives to make intercession for them.

a. **Also there were many priests**: The priesthood under the Law of Moses constantly changed, and so was better or worse through the years depending on the character of the priest. In contrast, Jesus **has an unchangeable priesthood**. Jesus will never die and has a *permanent* priesthood. We don't need to worry about a "bad priest" replacing Him.

b. **Continues forever**: This ancient Greek word has the idea of "remaining as a servant." Jesus **continues forever**, and He **continues** as a servant, even after He ascended into heaven.

c. **He is also able to save to the uttermost**: The unchanging nature of Jesus' priesthood means that the salvation He gives is also unchanging, permanent, and secure. Most people read this verse as if it says Jesus is **able to save** *from* **the uttermost**. But it really says Jesus is **able to save** *to* **the uttermost**. Because He is our High Priest **forever**, He can save *forever*.

i. The evangelist Billy Sunday had a great sermon, speaking passionately about how God saved him "from the gutter-most," because he was a gutter-drunk when God saved him. This was a great line from a great preacher, but it was not true to what the Bible says - we are saved not *from* but *to* the uttermost.

ii. "The verb 'to save' is used absolutely, which means that Christ will save in the most comprehensive sense; he saves from all that humanity needs saving from." (Morris)

d. **Those who come to God through Him**: This tells us *whom* Jesus is able to save. It means those who abide in the Son and have fellowship with the Father. It also shows where we have to come for salvation - **to God**. It is one thing to come to church; it is another thing to **come to God**.

i. This shows the place of *abiding* in the security of the believer. When we **come to God through Him**, He saves us **to the uttermost**. In Jesus there is complete security of salvation.

e. **He ever lives to make intercession for them**: It strengthens us to know that Jesus prays for us, and that **He ever lives to** pray for us. This is tremendous encouragement to anyone who feels like giving up.

i. Romans 8:33-34 shows that the Apostle Paul consider this intercessory work of Jesus on our behalf important. There, he pictured Jesus defending us against every charge or condemnation through His intercession.

ii. "Our blessed Lord is interceding for us, but He is in no sense appeasing God. All that God's holy Being and righteous government could demand was once for all, completely and forever, satisfied at the Cross." (Newell)

iii. Jesus' intercession on our behalf is not a matter of placating an angry Father who wants to destroy us. It is not a matter of continually chanting prayers on behalf of His people. It means that He continually represents us before the Father so that we can draw near through Him, and that He defends us against Satan's accusations and attacks.

iv. Luke 22:31-32 gives an example of Jesus' intercession for His people: *Simon, Simon! Indeed, Satan has asked for you, that he may sift you as wheat. But I have prayed for you, that your faith should not fail; and when you have returned to Me, strengthen your brethren.* Jesus prays to strengthen us in trials and seasons of attack, and against Satan's accusations.

4. (26-28) Jesus is better qualified to be a High Priest than any priest from the order of the Law of Moses.

For such a High Priest was fitting for us, *who is* holy, harmless, undefiled, separate from sinners, and has become higher than the heavens; who does not need daily, as those high priests, to offer up sacrifices, first for His own sins and then for the people's, for this He did once for all when He offered up Himself. For the law appoints as high priests men

who have weakness, but the word of the oath, which came after the law, *appoints* **the Son who has been perfected forever.**

a. **For such a High Priest was fitting for us**: The priests under the Law of Moses did not have the personal character of the Son of God. Jesus is **holy, harmless** (without guile or deception), **undefiled, separate from sinners** (in the sense of not sharing in their sin). Jesus is far superior in His personal character than any earthly priest.

> i. The believer should *glory* in these passages exalting Jesus and showing His superiority. "The superiority of our Lord Jesus Christ is a topic that will not interest everybody. To many persons it will seem a piece of devotional rapture, if not an idle tale. Yet there will ever be a remnant according to the election of grace to whom this meditation will be inexpressibly sweet." (Spurgeon)

b. **Has become higher than the heavens**: Two facts prove the perfect character of Jesus. First, His exaltation in heaven. Second, that He did not need to **offer up sacrifices, first for His own sins** - which the other priests needed to do **daily**.

c. **When He offered up Himself**: This is totally unique. A priest may bring a sacrifice and offer it on the altar. But Jesus was *both* the priest *and* the sacrifice. This is the *best* sacrifice brought to God the Father by the *best* priest.

> i. When He offered up Himself it was a *willing* offering. "Oh, this makes the sacrifice of Christ so blessed and glorious! They dragged the bullocks and they drove the sheep to the altar; they bound the calves with cords, even with cords to the altar's horn; but not so was it with the Christ of God. None did compel him to die; he laid down his life voluntarily, for he had power to lay it down, and to take it again." (Spurgeon)

d. **For the law appoints as high priests men who have weaknesses**: Under the Law of Moses the priests were always men with **weaknesses**. But Jesus is a **Son who has been perfected forever**. Because He is a perfect High Priest, He was able to **offer up Himself** as a perfect sacrifice for our sin. Jesus is *perfectly* qualified to be our *perfect* High Priest - **perfected forever**.

Hebrews 8 - A New, Better Covenant

A. Jesus, our heavenly priest.

1. (1-2) A summary of points previously made regarding Jesus as our High Priest.

Now *this is* the main point of the things we are saying: We have such a High Priest, who is seated at the right hand of the throne of the Majesty in the heavens, a Minister of the sanctuary and of the true tabernacle which the Lord erected, and not man.

a. **This is the main point of the things we are saying**: The writer of Hebrews brings together the **main point** of the previous chapter. We have a **High Priest** - Jesus Christ - who serves us from a position of all authority in heaven (**seated at the right hand of the throne of the Majesty**).

b. **Who is seated at the right hand of the throne**: Additionally, Jesus is **seated** in heaven, in contrast to the continual service of the priesthood under the Law of Moses.

i. The tabernacle and the temple of the Old Covenant had beautiful furnishings, but no place for the priests to *sit down* because their work was never finished. The work of Jesus *is* finished, therefore He **is seated** in heaven.

c. **A Minister of the sanctuary and of the true tabernacle**: Jesus doesn't serve as a priest in an earthly tabernacle or temple. He serves in the **true tabernacle which the Lord erected**, the **original** made by God. The tabernacle of Moses was a *copy* of this **original**, and it was made by man (Exodus 25:8-9).

i. Some suppose the **true tabernacle** is the Church or Jesus' earthly body. But it is best to understand it as the heavenly reality that the earthly tabernacle imitated.

2. (3) Jesus' priesthood had a sacrifice - and a better sacrifice.

For every high priest is appointed to offer both gifts and sacrifices. Therefore *it is* necessary that this One also have something to offer.

a. **Every high priest is appointed to offer both gifts and sacrifices**: Sacrifice for sin is essential to the concept of priesthood. Jesus represented a superior priesthood and offered a superior sacrifice. He laid down His own life to atone for sin.

b. **It is necessary that this One also have something to offer**: Though Jesus never offered a sacrifice according to the Law of Moses He did offer a better sacrifice - the sacrifice of Himself.

3. (4-5) Jesus' priesthood had a temple - and a better temple.

For if He were on earth, He would not be a priest, since there are priests who offer the gifts according to the law; who serve the copy and shadow of the heavenly things, as Moses was divinely instructed when he was about to make the tabernacle. For He said, "See *that* you make all things according to the pattern shown you on the mountain."

a. **If He were on earth, He would not be a priest**: Jesus was not qualified to serve in the inferior earthly priesthood. **There are priests** - plenty of them – who were qualified to serve in the priesthood according to the Law of Moses.

b. **Who serve the copy and shadow of the heavenly things**: There were plenty of priests who could serve in **the copy and shadow** on earth. Yet Jesus is the only One qualified to serve in the superior heavenly priesthood. The earthly service, though it was glorious in the eyes of man, was really only a **copy and shadow** of the superior heavenly service.

c. **Copy and shadow of the heavenly things**: Exodus 25:40 tells us that Moses' tabernacle built on earth was made according to a *pattern* that existed in heaven. This was the *pattern which was shown to you* [Moses] *on the mountain* (Exodus 25:40). Therefore, there is a **heavenly** temple that served as a pattern for the earthly tabernacle and temple. Jesus' ministry as our High Priest takes place in this **heavenly** temple, not in **the copy and shadow** built on earth.

i. First century Jews took tremendous pride in the temple and did so for good reason: it was a spectacular architectural achievement. However glorious the Jerusalem temple was, it was of man (and mostly built by Herod the Great, a corrupt and ungodly man). Therefore it was *nothing* compared to the glory of the heavenly temple that Jesus served in.

4. (6) The result: Jesus presides over a superior priesthood with a better covenant and better promises.

But now He has obtained a more excellent ministry, inasmuch as He is also Mediator of a better covenant, which was established on better promises.

a. **He has obtained a more excellent ministry**: No earthly priest could take away sin the way Jesus did. Therefore Jesus' **ministry** is far better than the ministry of the priesthood under the Law of Moses.

b. **Mediator of a better covenant**: Jesus has mediated for us a **better covenant**, a covenant of grace and not of works, guaranteed for us by a cosigner (Hebrews 7:22). It is a **covenant** marked by believing and receiving instead of by earning and deserving.

i. Jesus is our **Mediator** for this greater covenant. **Mediator** is the ancient Greek word *mesites*, which means "one who stands in the middle between two people and brings them together." (Barclay)

ii. Moses was the mediator of the Old Covenant because he "brought the two parties together." Jesus is the **Mediator** of the New Covenant, **a better covenant**, bringing us to God the Father.

iii. Jesus' covenant is **a better covenant**, better than any of the previous covenants God made with men. The covenant of Jesus fulfills the other covenants described in the Bible.

- There is an *eternal covenant* between the members of the Godhead that made possible the salvation of man (Hebrews 13:20).

- God's redemptive plan was continued through the covenant He made with *Abraham* (Genesis 12:1-3).

- The *Mosaic covenant* was another step in God's redemptive plan (Exodus 24:3-8).

- The *Davidic covenant* was yet another step in God's redemptive plan (2 Samuel 7:1-16).

- The redemptive plan of God was fulfilled in the *New Covenant* (Luke 22:14-20).

c. **Which was established on better promises**: Jesus has **better promises** for us. These are **promises** to see us through the most desperate and dark times. These are **promises** that become alive to us through the Spirit of God. These are **promises** of blessing and undeserved favor instead of promises to curse and judge.

B. The superiority of the New Covenant.

1. (7) The fact that God mentions another covenant is proves that there is something lacking in the Old Covenant.

For if that first *covenant* had been faultless, then no place would have been sought for a second.

> a. **If the first covenant had been faultless**: It is in the nature of man to come up with things that are "new" but not needed. God isn't like that. If God established a New Covenant, it means that there was something lacking in the Old Covenant.

2. (8-12) The New Covenant as it is presented in the Hebrew Scriptures (quoting from Jeremiah 31:31-34).

Because finding fault with them, He says: "Behold, the days are coming, says the LORD, when I will make a new covenant with the house of Israel and with the house of Judah—not according to the covenant that I made with their fathers in the day when I took them by the hand to lead them out of the land of Egypt; because they did not continue in My covenant, and I disregarded them, says the LORD. For this *is* the covenant that I will make with the house of Israel after those days, says the LORD: I will put My laws in their mind and write them on their hearts; and I will be their God, and they shall be My people. None of them shall teach his neighbor, and none his brother, saying, 'Know the LORD,' for all shall know Me, from the least of them to the greatest of them. For I will be merciful to their unrighteousness, and their sins and their lawless deeds I will remember no more."

> a. **Finding fault**: In this passage from Jeremiah 31, God shows that something was lacking in the Old Covenant - because a New Covenant was promised. In the days of Jeremiah the New Covenant was still in the future, because he wrote **"Behold the days are coming."**
>
> > i. In its context, Jeremiah's prophecy probably comes from the days of Josiah's renewal of the covenant after finding the law (2 Kings 23:3). This renewal was good, but it wasn't enough because Jeremiah looked forward to **a new covenant**.
>
> b. **I will make**: The Lord made it clear that this covenant would originate with God, and not with man. At Sinai under the Old Covenant the key words were *if you* (Exodus 19:5), but in the New Covenant, the key words are **I will**.
>
> c. **A new covenant**: This covenant is truly **new**, not merely "new and improved" in the way things are marketed to us today. Today, products are

said to be "new and improved" when there is no substantial difference in the product. But when God says "**new**," He means **new**.

> i. There are two ancient Greek words that describe the concept of "new." *Neos* described newness in regard to *time*. Something may be a copy of something old but if it recently made, it can be called *neos*. The ancient Greek word *kainos* (the word used here) described something that is not only **new** in reference to time, but is truly **new** in its quality. It isn't simply a new reproduction of something old.

d. **With the house of Israel and the house of Judah**: The New Covenant definitely began with Israel but it was never intended to end with Israel (Matthew 15:24 and Acts 1:8).

e. **Not according to the covenant that I made with their fathers**: This covenant is *not like* the **covenant** God made with **their fathers**. Again, this emphasizes that there is something substantially *different* about the New Covenant.

f. **Because they did not continue in My covenant**: The weakness of the Old Covenant was not in the Covenant itself. It was in the weakness and inability of man. The reason the Old Covenant didn't "work" was **because they did not continue in My covenant**.

g. **I will put My laws in their mind and write them on their hearts**: The New Covenant features transformation from within, not regulation through external law.

> i. The Old Covenant came in with such awe and terror that it should have made everyone obey out of fear. But they sinned against the Old Covenant almost immediately. The New Covenant works obedience through the law written **in their mind** and **on their hearts**.

h. **I will be their God, and they shall be My people**: The New Covenant also features a greater intimacy with God than what was available under the Old Covenant.

> i. "The best way to make a man keep a law is to make him love the law-giver." (Spurgeon)

i. **Their sins and lawless deeds I will remember no more**: The New Covenant offers a true, complete cleansing from sin, different and better than the mere "covering over" of sin in the Old Covenant.

3. (13) The significance of a *New* Covenant.

In that He says, "A new *covenant*," He has made the first obsolete. Now what is becoming obsolete and growing old is ready to vanish away.

a. **He has made the first obsolete**: Now that the New Covenant has been inaugurated, the Old Covenant is thereby **obsolete**.

b. **What is becoming obsolete and growing old is ready to vanish away**: The message was clear to these discouraged Christians from Jewish backgrounds, who thought of going back to a more Jewish faith. They simply *can't* go back to an inferior covenant, which was ready to completely **vanish away**.

i. The system of sacrifice under the Law of Moses soon did **vanish away** with the coming destruction of the Temple and the Roman destruction of Jerusalem.

Differences Between the Old Covenant and the New Covenant

1. They were instituted at different times.
   - The Old Covenant around 1446 B.C.
   - The New Covenant around A.D. 33

2. They were instituted at different places.
   - The Old Covenant at Mount Sinai
   - The New Covenant at Mount Zion

3. They were spoken in different ways.
   - The Old Covenant was thundered with fear and dread at Mount Sinai (Exodus 19:17-24)
   - Jesus Christ, God the Son, declared the New Covenant with love and grace

4. They have different mediators.
   - Moses mediated the Old Covenant
   - Jesus is the mediator of the New Covenant

5. They are different in their subject matter.
   - The Old Covenant *demanded* a covenant of works
   - The New Covenant *fulfills* the covenant of works through the completed work of Jesus

6. They are different in how they were dedicated.
   - The Old Covenant was dedicated with the blood of animals sprinkled on the people (Exodus 24:5-8)
   - The New Covenant was dedicated with Jesus' blood (signifying His sacrificial death) spiritually applied to His people

7. They are different in their priests.
   - The Old Covenant is represented by the priesthood of the Law of Moses and high priests descended from Aaron
   - The New Covenant has a priesthood of all believers and a High Priest according to the order of Melchizedek

8. They are different in their sacrifices.
   - The Old Covenant demanded endless repetition of imperfect sacrifices
   - The New Covenant provides a once and for all, perfect sacrifice of the Son of God Himself

9. They are different in how and where they were written.
   - The Old Covenant was written by God on tablets of stone
   - The New Covenant is written by God on the hearts of His people

10. They are different in their goals.
    - The goal of the Old Covenant was to discover sin, to condemn it, and to set a "fence" around it
    - The goal of the New Covenant is to declare the love, grace, and mercy of God, and to give repentance, remission of sin, and eternal life

11. They are different in their practical effect on living.
    - The Old Covenant ends in bondage (through no fault of its own)
    - The New Covenant provides true liberty

12. They are different in their giving of the Holy Spirit.
    - Under the Old Covenant the Holy Spirit was given to certain people for certain specific duties
    - Under the New Covenant the Holy Spirit is poured out freely on all who will receive Him by faith

13. They are different in their idea of the Kingdom of God.
    - Under the Old Covenant, the Kingdom of God is mainly seen as the supreme rule of Israel over the nations
    - Under the New Covenant, the Kingdom of God is both a present spiritual reality and a coming literal fact

14. They are different in their substance.

- The Old Covenant has vivid shadows
- The New Covenant has the reality

15. They are different in the extent of their administration.

- The Old Covenant was confined to the descendants of Abraham through Isaac and Jacob according to the flesh
- The New Covenant is extended to all nations and races under heaven

16. They are different in what they actually accomplish.

- The Old Covenant made nothing perfect
- The New Covenant can and will bring in the perfection of God's people

17. They are different in their duration.

- The Old Covenant was designed to prepare the way for the New Covenant and then pass away as a principle of God's dealing with men
- The New Covenant was designed to last forever

"Let us observe from these things, that the state of the gospel, or of the Church under the New Testament, being accompanied by the highest privileges and advantages that it is capable of in this world, there is a great obligation on all believers unto holiness and fruitfulness in obedience, unto the glory of God; and the heinousness of their sin, by whom this covenant is neglected or despised, is abundantly manifested." (John Owen)

Hebrews 9 - The Old Covenant and the New Covenant Compared

A. Features of the Old Covenant described.

1. (1-5) The Old Covenant's tabernacle and its furnishings.

Then indeed, even the first *covenant* had ordinances of divine service and the earthly sanctuary. For a tabernacle was prepared: the first *part*, in which *was* the lampstand, the table, and the showbread, which is called the sanctuary; and behind the second veil, the part of the tabernacle which is called the Holiest of All, which had the golden censer and the ark of the covenant overlaid on all sides with gold, in which *were* the golden pot that had the manna, Aaron's rod that budded, and the tablets of the covenant; and above it were the cherubim of glory overshadowing the mercy seat. Of these things we cannot now speak in detail.

a. **The earthly sanctuary**: The tabernacle ordained by the Old Covenant was planned by God, but planned for an **earthly** service.

b. **For a tabernacle was prepared**: The **tabernacle** was a tent 45 feet (15 meters) long, 15 feet (5 meters) wide, and 15 feet (5 meters) high, divided into two rooms. The larger room (**the first part**) was a 15 feet (5 meter) by 30 feet (10 meter) "holy place." **Behind the second veil** was the smaller room was a 15 feet (5 meter) by 15 feet (5 meter), called **the Holiest of All**.

c. **The lampstand**: This setting for the lamps of the tabernacle had a middle stem and six branches stood in **the first part**. It was of an unspecified size, made of pure gold and provided the only *light* for the tabernacle (Exodus 25:31-40).

d. **The table**: This sat in **the first part** and was made of acacia wood covered with gold, 3 feet long, 1½ feet wide, and 2 feet 3 inches high. It held twelve loaves of **showbread**, each representing God's fellowship with the twelve tribes of Israel (Exodus 25:23-30).

e. **The sanctuary**: This refers to **the first part**, known as the "holy place." A **veil** (a thick curtain) separated **the first part** from the **Holiest of All**, also known as the "holy of holies" (Exodus 26:31-33).

f. **The golden altar of incense**: This was made of acacia wood covered with gold, 1½ feet (½ meter) square, and 3 feet (1 meter) high. It stood at the veil before the "holy of holies" and was used to burn incense (Exodus 30:1-8).

g. **The ark of the covenant**: This stood inside the **Holiest of All** and was a chest made of acacia wood covered with gold, 3¾ feet long, 2¼ feet wide, and 2¼ feet high, with rings for polls along its side to carry it without touching the ark itself (Exodus 25:10-22).

> i. Inside the ark were **the golden pot that had the manna** (Exodus 16:33), **Aaron's rod that budded** (Numbers 17:6-11), and **the tablets of the covenant** (Exodus 25:16).
>
> - The **manna** reminded Israel of God's provision and their ungratefulness.
> - **Aaron's rod** reminded Israel of their rebellion against God's authority.
> - The **tablets of the covenant** reminded Israel of their failure to keep the Ten Commandments and rest of the law.

h. **The mercy seat**: This was the ornate "lid" for the ark of the covenant, made with the designs of cherubim upon it. The blood of sacrifice was sprinkled upon it for the forgiveness of Israel's sin on the Day of Atonement (Exodus 25:17-22).

> i. As God looked down into the ark, He saw the symbols of Israel's sin, rebellion and failure. But when the blood of sacrifice was applied to the mercy seat, the blood of sacrifice covered His sight of the sin of Israel.

2. (6-7) Priestly service in the tabernacle under the Old Covenant.

Now when these things had been thus prepared, the priests always went into the first part of the tabernacle, performing *the services*. But into the second part the high priest *went* alone once a year, not without blood, which he offered for himself and *for* the people's sins *committed* in ignorance;

> a. **The priests always went into the first part of the tabernacle, performing the services**: The **priests**, as appointed, went daily into the holy place to perform priestly functions such as tending the lampstand and replacing the showbread.

b. **But into the second part the high priest went alone once a year**: The **second part** – sometimes knows as the "holy of holies" – was entered only **once a year** by the high priest **alone**, on the Day of Atonement.

c. **The high priest went alone once a year, not without blood**: His entrance into the **second part** was not for fellowship, but only for atonement. The atoning **blood** was first for his own sins and then for the sins of his people.

> i. Access into the *Holiest of All* was thus severely restricted. Even when someone could enter, it wasn't for real fellowship with God.

> ii. The ancient Jewish Rabbis wrote of how the high priest did not prolong his prayer in the Holy of Holies on the Day of Atonement, because it might make the people think he had been killed. When he came out he threw a party for all his friends, because he had emerged safely from the presence of God.

d. **The people's sins committed in ignorance**: Sins of **ignorance** were the specific aim of the Day of Atonement. It was assumed that *known* sin would be taken care of through the regular sin offerings and the daily sacrifices.

> i. In this respect, Jesus' work is far greater than the work done on the Day of Atonement. Jesus' work on the cross is sufficient to atone for both the sins we do in ignorance and sins that we know.

3. (8-10) The Holy Spirit gives understanding regarding the priestly service under the Old Covenant.

The Holy Spirit indicating this, that the way into the Holiest of All was not yet made manifest while the first tabernacle was still standing. It *was* symbolic for the present time in which both gifts and sacrifices are offered which cannot make him who performed the service perfect in regard to the conscience; *concerned* only with foods and drinks, various washings, and fleshly ordinances imposed until the time of reformation.

a. **The way into the Holiest of All was not yet made manifest while the first tabernacle was still standing**: The old had to pass away before God's new way could be revealed.

b. **It was symbolic for the present time**: **Symbolic** is the ancient Greek word *parabole*. The tabernacle itself and all that the Old Covenant represented were suggestive of deeper truths, *parables* of the New Covenant.

c. **Cannot make him who performed the service perfect in regard to the conscience**: The priestly service under the Old Covenant could not make the priests offering those sacrifices perfect and clean in **regard to the conscience**.

i. If the cleansing is incomplete for the priest, how much more for the person the priest worked on behalf of!

c. **Fleshly ordinances imposed until the time of reformation**: The weakness of the priestly service under the Old Covenant was its inability to address the need for inner transformation in man. Therefore it was only **imposed until the time of reformation**.

B. Features of the New Covenant described.

1. (11) The superior sanctuary of the New Covenant.

But Christ came *as* High Priest of the good things to come, with the greater and more perfect tabernacle not made with hands, that is, not of this creation.

a. **The greater and more perfect tabernacle not made with hands**: Jesus, as our High Priest, ministers in a superior sanctuary - the very throne room of God. This is obviously a place greater than anything human **hands** could make.

2. (12-15) The superior sacrifice of the New Covenant.

Not with the blood of goats and calves, but with His own blood He entered the Most Holy Place once for all, having obtained eternal redemption. For if the blood of bulls and goats and the ashes of a heifer, sprinkling the unclean, sanctifies for the purifying of the flesh, how much more shall the blood of Christ, who through the eternal Spirit offered Himself without spot to God, cleanse your conscience from dead works to serve the living God? And for this reason He is the Mediator of the new covenant, by means of death, for the redemption of the transgressions under the first covenant, that those who are called may receive the promise of the eternal inheritance.

a. **The blood of goats and calves**: Animal sacrifice was sufficient for a temporary covering of sin, but only a perfect sacrifice could obtain **eternal redemption**.

i. Jesus' sacrifice was superior in that it was *perfect, voluntary, rational,* and *motivated by love.*

b. **With His own blood He entered the Most Holy Place once for all**: At the tabernacle, the sacrifice was made outside the veil, at the altar; but the atoning blood was brought into the most holy place, which represent the throne of God. In the same pattern Jesus had to die *here*, outside heaven and among sinful men, but the payment his death made had to be satisfied in heaven itself.

i. **He entered the Most Holy Place**: The High Priest entered once a year, going through the veil and back again, letting the veil fall behind him as he left – the barrier remained. Jesus tore the veil, and stays *in* the most holy place, heaven itself, welcoming us in. This is what makes Christianity all about *access*, not *barriers*.

ii. **With His own blood**: "Blood in Scripture always includes the two thoughts of a death suffered and a life offered." (Thomas)

iii. "The Lord Jesus Christ did not come to earth to make a reconciliation by the holiness of his life, or by the earnestness of his teaching, but by his death." (Spurgeon)

iv. "The Lord Jesus did not bring before God the sufferings of others or the merits of others, but his own life and death." (Spurgeon)

c. **For if the blood of bulls and goats... sanctifies for the purifying of the flesh, how much more shall the blood of Christ**: If these imperfect sacrifices were received as sufficient by Israel, then they should much more regard the ultimate sufficiency of the perfect sacrifice.

i. The **ashes of a heifer** refer to the remains of a burnt offering that was preserved. The ashes were sprinkled in the laver of washing to provide water suitable for ceremonial cleansing (Numbers 19:1-10).

ii. This was a shadow, fulfilled and done away with when Jesus offered a perfect cleansing. Therefore there is no value in "holy water" used by the Roman Catholic Church.

iii. Reportedly, there is a search for a "red heifer" that can be sacrificed, and its ashes used as part or a restoration of priestly functions for a rebuilt temple in Jerusalem.

d. **How much more shall the blood of Christ... cleanse your conscience from dead works to serve the living God?** The sacrifice of Jesus is sufficient to even restore our damaged **conscience**.

i. Our **conscience** is a wonderful tool from God. But it isn't perfect. Our conscience can be *seared* (1 Timothy 4:2). Our conscience can be *defiled* (Titus 1:15). Our conscience can be *evil* (Hebrews 10:22).

e. **Cleanse your conscience from dead works**: The idea behind **dead works** is probably of sin in general, in the sense of "works that bring death." But it must also speak to the vain continuation of Old Covenant sacrifice, which is certainly a **dead work** - and the very type of thing these discouraged Jewish Christians were tempted to go back to.

f. **To serve the living God**: The believer is cleansed, conscience and all, not to live unto himself but **to serve the living God**. The ancient Greek word translated **serve** here is *latreuo*, which speaks of religious or ceremonial, priestly service.

> i. "And, dear friends, do keep in mind that you are henceforth to 'serve the living God.' You that are acquainted with the Greek will find that the kind of service here mentioned is not that which the slave or servant renders to his master, but a worshipful service such as priests render unto God. We that have been purged by Christ are to render to God the worship of a royal priesthood. It is ours to present prayers, thanksgivings, and sacrifice; it is ours to offer the incense of intercession; it is ours to light the lamp of testimony and furnish the table of shewbread." (Spurgeon)

g. **He is the Mediator of the new covenant, by means of death**: Jesus' work as a Mediator is fundamentally accomplished at His **death**. His heavenly work of mediation looks back to that perfect sacrifice.

h. **For the redemption of the transgressions under the first covenant**: Jesus' payment on the cross accomplished **redemption** for those under the **first covenant**. Every sacrifice for sin made in faith under the Mosaic command was an IOU paid in full at the cross.

3. (16-22) The necessity of Jesus' death.

For where there *is* a testament, there must also of necessity be the death of the testator. For a testament *is* in force after men are dead, since it has no power at all while the testator lives. Therefore not even the first *covenant* was dedicated without blood. For when Moses had spoken every precept to all the people according to the law, he took the blood of calves and goats, with water, scarlet wool, and hyssop, and sprinkled both the book itself and all the people, saying, "This *is* the blood of the covenant which God has commanded you." Then likewise he sprinkled with blood both the tabernacle and all the vessels of the ministry. And according to the law almost all things are purified with blood, and without shedding of blood there is no remission.

a. **For a testament is in force after men are dead**: A **testament** (in the sense of a "last will and testament") only takes effect when the person who made the testament dies. Therefore Jesus had to die for the testament - the covenant - to take effect.

> i. "The same word in the Greek is used for 'covenant' and 'testament,' and although the double use is difficult, there seems to be no doubt that in verse 15 the word means 'covenant,' and in verses 16 and 17 'testament,' and then in verse 18 'covenant' again." (Thomas)

ii. "If there be a question about whether a man is alive or not, you cannot administer to his estate, but when you have certain evidence that the testator has died then the will stands. So is it with the blessed gospel: if Jesus did not die, then the gospel is null and void." (Spurgeon)

b. **Therefore not even the first covenant was dedicated without blood**: Clearly, death was necessary to the Old Covenant. Virtually every part of the sacrificial system under the Law of Moses was touched by **blood** in some way or another.

c. **Without shedding of blood there is no remission**: This is a foundational principle of God's dealings with men. Modern people think that sin is remitted (forgiven) by *time*, by *our good works*, by our *decent lives*, or by simply *death*. But there is **no** forgiveness without the shedding of blood, and there is no *perfect* forgiveness without a *perfect* sacrifice.

i. The shedding of Jesus' blood is God's *answer* to man's problem of sin. In his sermon *The Blood-Shedding*, Spurgeon began by showing us three fools. The first is a soldier wounded on the field of battle. The medic comes to the soldier, and immediate the solider wants to know everything about the rifle and the soldier that shot him. The second fool is a ship captain, whose ship is about to go under in a terrible storm. The captain is not at the wheel of the ship, trying to guide it through the crashing waves; he is in his room studying charts, trying to determine where the storm came from. The third fool is a man who is sick and dying with sin, about to go under the waves of God's justice, yet is deeply troubled about the *origin* of evil. We should look to the *solution* more than to the problem.

4. (23-28) The perfect sanctuary receives a perfect sacrifice.

Therefore *it was* necessary that the copies of the things in the heavens should be purified with these, but the heavenly things themselves with better sacrifices than these. For Christ has not entered the holy places made with hands, *which are* copies of the true, but into heaven itself, now to appear in the presence of God for us; not that He should offer Himself often, as the high priest enters the Most Holy Place every year with blood of another—He then would have had to suffer often since the foundation of the world; but now, once at the end of the ages, He has appeared to put away sin by the sacrifice of Himself. And as it is appointed for men to die once, but after this the judgment, so Christ was offered once to bear the sins of many. To those who eagerly wait for Him He will appear a second time, apart from sin, for salvation.

a. **It was necessary that the copies of the things in the heavens should be purified with these**: It was acceptable for the **copies of the things**

in the heavens in the earthly sanctuary to be "purified" with imperfect sacrifices. But the **heavenly things themselves** could only be **purified** with a perfect offering.

> i. "*Purification* implies, not only cleansing from defilement, but also *dedication* or *consecration*. All the utensils employed in the tabernacle service were thus *purified* though incapable of any moral pollution." (Clarke)

b. **For Christ has not entered the holy places made with hands... but into heaven itself:** Jesus' sacrifice was made on earth, but it is the basis for His continuing work as our mediator and High Priest in heaven. The writer to the Hebrews proclaims it: **now to appear in the presence of God for us**. It's not hard to believe that Jesus does **appear in the presence of God**. But to believe that He appears there **for us** is glorious!

c. **Not that He should offer Himself often**: Jesus' ministry **for us** continues in heaven, *but not in the sense of continuing to atone for our sin*. His ministry continues **for us** in intercession and defending us against the accuser of God's people (Revelation 12:10). But it does **not** continue in the sense that **He should offer Himself often**. His sacrifice was once-for-all, and perfectly satisfied God's holy justice.

> i. This passage and principle is a direct rebuke to the Roman Catholic *practice* and *theology* of the mass. In the mass, the Roman Catholic Church desires to *repeat* - not remember, but *repeat* - the atoning sacrifice of Jesus innumerable times. This is absolutely indefensible Scripturally, and *denies* the finished work of Jesus Christ on the cross. The Scriptures make it plain: **not that He should offer Himself often**.

d. **He then would have had to suffer often since the foundation of the world**: If the sacrifice of Jesus were not *perfect*, then it would have to be *continual* and *constant* - even **since the foundation of the world**. Imperfect sacrifices must be repeated continually but a perfect sacrifice can be made once for all time, and genuinely **put away sin** (not just *cover* sin, as with sacrifice under the Old Covenant). The message is clear: **He has appeared to put away sin by the sacrifice of Himself**.

> i. This principle of sacrifice explains why the suffering of hell *must* be eternal for those who reject the atoning work of Jesus. They are in hell to pay the penalty of their sin, but as imperfect beings they are unable to make a perfect payment. If the payment is not perfect, then it has to be *continual* and *constant* - indeed, for all eternity. A soul could be released from hell the moment its debt of sin was completely paid - which is another way of saying *never*.

e. **And as it is appointed for men to die once, but after this the judgment, so Christ was offered once to bear the sins of many**: Just as certainly as we **die once** and then face **judgment**, so Jesus only had to die **once** (not repeatedly, not continually) to **bear** our sins.

i. It is not the intention of the writer to the Hebrews to discuss the issue of reincarnation. That is a side issue; he simply brings up the obvious point, **it is appointed for men to die once, but after this the judgment**. Just as that is obvious, so it is plain that **Christ was offered once to bear the sins of many**. For the writer to the Hebrews, the truth that **it is appointed for men to die once, but after this the judgment** is an indisputable principle.

ii. "A man dies once, and after that everything is fixed and settled, and he answers for his doings at the judgment. One life, one death - then everything is weighed, and the result declared: 'after this the judgment.' So Christ comes, and dies once; and after this, for him also the result of what he has done, namely, the salvation of those who look for him. He dies once, and then reaps the fixed result, according to the analogy of the human race, of which he became a member and representative." (Spurgeon)

iii. Though it was not really the point of the writer to the Hebrews to discuss reincarnation, he certainly and completely *denies* it here. We do not die and live and die and live, facing an eternal reckoning some number of lives down the road. This life is it, and then we face judgment. This means that *there are no second chances beyond the grave. Now* is the time to choose for Jesus Christ, because when we **die** we simply face **the judgment**.

iv. It is important to note that the principle of **it is appointed for men to die once** is not an *absolute principle*. There are some unique, remarkable exceptions. Enoch (Genesis 5:24) and Elijah (2 Kings 2:11) never *died once*. Several people in the Bible were raised from the dead (1 Kings 17:22, 2 Kings 13:20-21, Matthew 9:25, John 11:43-44, Acts 20:9-11), and therefore *died twice*. Those taken in the rapture (1 Thessalonians 4:17) will never *die once*. Yet these remarkable, unique exceptions do not deny the principle of **it is appointed for men to die once**; they are *exceptions that prove the rule*.

f. **He will appear a second time, apart from sin, for salvation**: The focus of Jesus' first coming was to deal with the sin problem through His atoning sacrifice. But now, having dealt with the sin problem perfectly, He comes again **apart from sin** - for the **salvation** (in the sense of *rescue*) of His people.

i. **To those who eagerly wait for Him**: It is *assumed* that all believers will **eagerly wait for Him**. It's a sad case that this assumption doesn't always play out as true.

ii. "It ought to be a daily disappointment when our Lord does not come; instead of being, as I fear it is, a kind of foregone conclusion that he will not come just yet." (Spurgeon)

Hebrews 10 - Holding Fast with a Perfect Sacrifice

A. The once for all sacrifice of Jesus.

1. (1-4) Sacrifice under the Old Covenant could not truly take away sin.

For the law, having a shadow of the good things to come, *and* not the very image of the things, can never with these same sacrifices, which they offer continually year by year, make those who approach perfect. For then would they not have ceased to be offered? For the worshipers, once purified, would have had no more consciousness of sins. But in those *sacrifices there is* a reminder of sins every year. For *it is* not possible that the blood of bulls and goats could take away sins.

a. **Having a shadow of the good things to come**: The Old Covenant (**the law**) was a mere **shadow** of the substance that is the New Covenant (also in Colossians 2:17 and Hebrews 8:5). **Shadow** means that the law communicated the outline and the figure of the fulfillment to come in Jesus, but was **not the very image of the things**.

i. **Shadow** isn't a bad thing. Sometimes a **shadow** can tell you a lot. But the **shadow** is not the substance. The Old Covenant and its law were not themselves bad or evil, they are only *incomplete* and *insufficient* to bring total cleansing from sin, and to save. The **shadow... can never... make those who approach perfect.**

ii. Newell notes that here the law is called a **shadow** and **not the very image of the things** - it is *not* an *eikon*. "An image, or *eikon*, like a good statue or a photograph, reveals features and facts accurately. This a shadow cannot do... Now **The Law** had *only* **shadows**." (Newell)

iii. "For example, you need a load of wood: you go to the wood man, and he takes you to a large oak tree in the far corner of the lot. Pointing to the long shadow it casts, he offers to sell you this *shadow*. Will you take it? Now, if God says that in the Law there was a *shadow*, not even the very image of the things - and of course, not the things themselves, why will you hold to the shadow?" (Newell)

iv. "When the sun is behind, the shadow is before; when the sun is before, the shadow is behind. So was it in Christ to them of old. The Sun was behind, and therefore the law or shadow was before; to us under grace the Sun is before, and now the ceremonies of the law, these shadows, are behind you, vanished away." (Trapp)

v. "In effect he is saying: 'Without Christ you cannot get beyond the shadows of God.'" (Barclay) **The very image**: The ancient Greek word *eikon* "Suggests what is in itself substantial and also gives a true representation of that which it images." (Dods)

b. **Would they not have ceased to be offered?** The writer to the Hebrews repeats a familiar argument: the *repetition* of sacrifice shows its inherent *weakness*. If animal sacrifices had solved the sin problem, then they could **have ceased to be offered**.

c. **For the worshipers, once purified, would have had no more consciousness of sins. But in those sacrifices there is a reminder of sins every year**: Every repeated sacrifice was a **reminder of sins**. It brought the **consciousness of sins** to the people again and again. But the work of Jesus on the cross *takes away sin*!

i. "All they are is *a reminder of sin*. So far from purifying a man, they remind him that he is not purified and that his sins still stand between him and God." (Barclay)

ii. "An atonement that needs constant repetition does not really atone; a conscience which has to be cleansed once a year has never been truly cleansed." (Robinson)

d. **For it is not possible that the blood of bulls and goats could take away sins**: Animal sacrifice under the Old Covenant could *cover* sin. The Hebrew word for *atonement* is *kophar*, which literally means, "to cover." Yet animal sacrifice could never **take away sins**. Only Jesus, the Perfect Sacrifice of the New Covenant, takes sins **away**.

i. "There was a kind of priestly tread-mill of sacrifice...There was no end to this process and it left men still conscious of their sin and alienated from God." (Barclay)

ii. "'Take away' (*aphaireo*) is used of a literal taking off, as in Peter's cutting off the ear of the high priest's slave (Luke 22:50), or metaphorically as of the removal of reproach (Luke 1:25). It signifies the complete removal of sin so that it is no longer a factor in the situation. That is what is needed and that is what the sacrifices could not provide." (Morris)

iii. "Hering, for example, points out that this distinguishes Christianity from the mystery religions, where the sacrifice of the god was repeated annually. In fact, there is no other religion in which one great happening brings salvation through the centuries and throughout the world. This is the distinctive doctrine of Christianity." (Morris)

2. (5-10) Psalm 40:6-8 gives a prophetic foundation for Jesus' perfect sacrifice under the New Covenant.

Therefore, when He came into the world, He said:

"Sacrifice and offering You did not desire,
But a body You have prepared for Me.
In burnt offerings and *sacrifices* for sin
You had no pleasure.
Then I said, 'Behold, I have come—
In the volume of the book it is written of Me—
To do Your will, O God.'"

Previously saying, "Sacrifice and offering, burnt offerings, and *offerings* for sin You did not desire, nor had pleasure *in them*" (which are offered according to the law), then He said, "Behold, I have come to do Your will, O God." He takes away the first that He may establish the second. By that will we have been sanctified through the offering of the body of Jesus Christ once *for all*.

a. **He said**: This quotation is taken from the Septuagint version of Psalm 40:6-8 (the Septuagint is the ancient Greek translation of the Old Testament that was the most commonly used Bible in the first century). It shows that prophetically Jesus declared the insufficient character of Old Covenant sacrifice and declared His willingness to offer a perfect sacrifice under the New Covenant.

i. "The text of the LXX is followed in the main which differs from the Hebrew chiefly in having *sōma* (body) rather than *ōtia* (ears)." (Robertson)

b. **Sacrifice and offering You did not desire**: More animal sacrifices, made under the law, would not please God. Repeatedly in the Old Testament God expressed His desire for obedience rather than sacrifice.

i. **Sacrifice and offering....burnt offerings and sacrifices for sin**: "It is probable that the four terms which the psalmist uses for sacrifice are intended to cover all the main types of offering prescribed in the Levitical ritual." (Bruce)

c. **But a body You have prepared for Me**: Instead, what pleased God could only come through Jesus, the incarnate Son of God. In the incarnation the body of Jesus was perfectly **prepared** and suited to live as fully man and fully God.

i. "There is no question that the author is convinced about the reality of the pre-existence of Christ." (Guthrie)

ii. "His incarnation itself is viewed as an act of submission to God's will and, as such, an anticipation of His supreme submission to that will in death." (Bruce)

d. **Behold, I have come... to do Your will, O God**: Jesus' submission to God's the Father's will had its ultimate fulfillment in His obedience to the cross. This desire to do God's will was shown in the Garden of Gethsemane (Luke 22:39-44) and fulfilled at the cross.

i. "*To do thy will, O God* is the aim of the perfect man. It has only partially been fulfilled by even the most pious of men, except by Jesus. What was seen as the most desirable aim by the psalmist, becomes an expression of fact on the lips of Jesus." (Guthrie)

e. **Behold, I have come to do Your will, O God**: The sacrifice of Jesus was determined before the foundation of the world (1 Peter 1:20; Revelation 13:8). Yet it was still an act of His **will** to submit to the incarnation and the cross at the appointed time; **by that will we have been sanctified through the offering of the body of Jesus Christ**.

i. Our sanctification - our being set apart to God - is founded on the **will** of Jesus, not our own will. It is founded on the **offering** of Jesus, not on our own offering or sacrifices for God.

f. **Once for all**: These are the important words of this passage, and the writer to the Hebrews repeats the theme over and over again: **once for all**.

i. "The one sacrifice does the work that the many failed to do. One wonders how priests who claim that the 'mass' is the sacrifice of Christ's body repeated explain this verse." (Robertson)

ii. "The heavenly high priest has indeed a continual ministry to discharge on His people's behalf at the Father's right hand; but that is the ministry of intercession on the basis of the sacrifice presented and accepted once and for all, it is not the constant or repeated offering of His sacrifice. This last misconception has no doubt been fostered in the Western Church by a defective Vulgate rendering which springs from a well-known inadequacy of the Latin verb." (Bruce)

3. (11-18) The finished work of Jesus Christ.

And every priest stands ministering daily and offering repeatedly the same sacrifices, which can never take away sins. But this Man, after He had offered one sacrifice for sins forever, sat down at the right hand of God, from that time waiting till His enemies are made His footstool. For by one offering He has perfected forever those who are being sanctified. But the Holy Spirit also witnesses to us; for after He had said before, "This *is* the covenant that I will make with them after those days, says the LORD: I will put My laws into their hearts, and in their minds I will write them," *then He adds,* "Their sins and their lawless deeds I will remember no more." Now where there is remission of these, *there is* no longer an offering for sin.

a. **Every priest stands ministering daily**: The priests had to *stand* continually in their work. Their work continued **daily** and sacrifices had to be **repeatedly** offered. The priests could never sit down! In contrast, Jesus **sat down at the right hand of God**, having finished His work of sacrificing for sin.

i. **But this Man**: "Opposed to the plurality of Levitical priests. One sacrifice, and once for ever, not many and often, as they." (Trapp)

ii. The sacrifices under the Old Covenant could never cure the sin problem, left us as a patient who continually needed the medicine, or like a weed that only has its head plucked out, not the root.

iii. In contrast, the seated posture of Jesus is important. It shows that His work is finished. He doesn't need to stand **ministering daily and offering repeatedly the same sacrifices** as priests under the Old Covenant had to. Jesus still ministers in heaven - He has a ministry of intercession for His people. But that ministry flows from His completed work, so He can adopt a posture of *rest* - He **sat down at the right hand of God**.

iv. Spurgeon pointed out that the comma can be placed differently in the sentence, **after He had offered one sacrifice for sins forever, sat down at the right hand of God**. It is possible to translate, **after He had offered one sacrifice for sins, forever sat down at the right hand of God**. Either one is permitted and either one is correct, though the common translation is probably preferred.

v. When Jesus claimed the place at the right hand of God, the high priest regarded it as blasphemy – as Jesus claiming to be God Himself (Mark 14:62-63).

b. **Till His enemies are made His footstool**: This looks forward to the consummation of the work of Jesus, and every part connects. The incarnation leads to His perfect life; His perfect life leads to His atoning death; His atoning death leads to His resurrection; His resurrection leads to His ascension to glory; His ascension to glory leads to His return and triumph over every enemy.

c. **He has perfected forever those who are being sanctified**: This makes it plain that the work of Jesus is effective only for **those who are being sanctified**. The work of Jesus is *capable* of saving every human being, but it is only *effective* in saving **those who are being sanctified** (set apart to God).

> i. "What a glorious word! Those for whom Christ has died were perfected by his death. It does not mean that he made them perfect in characters so that they are no longer sinners, but that he made those for whom he died perfectly free from the guilt of sin. When Christ took their sins upon himself, sin remained no longer upon them, for it could not be in two places at one and the same time." (Spurgeon)

d. **The Holy Spirit also witnesses to us... says the LORD**: In this passage, the writer to the Hebrews clearly shows that the **Holy Spirit** is **the LORD**, *Yahweh* of the Old Testament. When the **Holy Spirit** speaks, the **LORD** speaks.

> i. "We have the threefold revelation of God in this passage, a very definite spiritual and practical exemplification of the Holy Trinity, in the *will* of God (Hebrews 10:9), the *work* of Christ (Hebrews 10:12), and the *witness* of the Spirit (Hebrews 10:15)." (Thomas)

e. **This is the covenant**: In the passage quoted from Jeremiah, the writer to the Hebrews makes note of the promises of the new **covenant**, instituted by the Messiah.

> i. **I will make with them after those days**: The new covenant is *new*. It comes **after those days**.

> ii. **I will put My laws into their hearts**: The new covenant has to do with an *inner transformation*. God changes the heart of man, and writes His law **into their hearts**.

> iii. **Their sins and their lawless deeds I will remember no more**: The new covenant offers *complete forgiveness*. The forgiveness is so complete that God can say that doesn't even **remember** our sins in light of the new covenant!

> iv. The Christian must endeavor to do with their sin exactly what God has done: forget about it. As well, this reminds us that the believer is *in*

no way on probation. Before God his past sin has no bearing on God's present dealing.

v. "Forgiveness of sin is the characteristic of the new covenant. In Jeremiah complete pardon of sins is promised. If the pardon is complete, there is left no place for the Levitical sacrifices under the new covenant." (Vincent)

f. **Now where there is remission of these, there is no longer an offering for sin**: Where sins are really forgiven and forgotten (**remission of these**), there no longer must be an offering for sin.

i. "In the words, **No more offering for sin**, we reach the conclusion of the doctrinal part of this great epistle to the **Hebrews**." (Newell) What follows after is mainly *exhortation*.

ii. "The Christ who died on Calvary's cross, will not have to die again for my new sins, or to offer a fresh atonement for any transgressions that I may yet commit. No; but, once for all, gathering up the whole mass of his people's sins into one colossal burden, he took it upon his shoulders, and flung the whole of it into the sepulcher wherein Once he slept, and there it is buried, never to be raised again to bear witness against the redeemed any more for ever." (Spurgeon)

iii. The work of Jesus for atonement is *finished*. If it is not enough for us, then nothing will be. "God has set forth Christ for you as guilty sinners to rest on; and if that is not enough for you, what more would you have? Christ has offered himself, and died and suffered in our stead, and gone into his glory; and, if you cannot depend upon him, what more would you have him do? Shall he come and die again? You have rejected him once; you would reject him though he died twice." (Spurgeon)

B. Encouraging the discouraged in light of Jesus' perfect sacrifice.

1. (19-21) A summary of what Jesus did for His people.

Therefore, brethren, having boldness to enter the Holiest by the blood of Jesus, by a new and living way which He consecrated for us, through the veil, that is, His flesh, and *having* a High Priest over the house of God,

a. **Having boldness**: This is stated as a fact, not an exhortation. We have access for a bold approach to God. The point is simple: we must take advantage of this access, and take it with **boldness**. On the Day of Atonement, the high priest entered the holiest place of all with fear and trembling, but we can **enter the Holiest** with **boldness**.

i. We can have **boldness** because we **enter the Holiest by the blood of Jesus**. If we entered as the Old Testament high priest did, with the blood of animals, we wouldn't have **boldness**. But with the **blood of Jesus** providing **a new and living way which He consecrated with us**, we really can come into the presence of God with **boldness**.

ii. This **boldness** is a complete contrast to the way the High Priest entered the Holy Place under the Old Covenant. "He went with fear and trembling, because, if he had neglected the smallest item prescribed by the law, he could expect nothing but death. Genuine believers can come even to the throne of God with confidence, as they carry into the Divine presence the infinitely meritorious blood of the great atonement; and, being justified through that blood, they have a right to all the blessings of the eternal kingdom." (Clarke)

iii. **Having boldness to enter**: "Special notice should be taken of the word 'having,' which, as elsewhere, always implies a present and conscious experience. It is impossible to exaggerate the 'present tenses of the blessed life,' of which this is one." (Thomas)

b. **A new and living way**: This means that the sacrifice of Jesus is *always fresh* in the mind of God. Though it happened centuries ago it is not "stale." It means that a **living** Jesus ushers us into the presence of God.

i. Newell on **a new and living way**: "It is eternally as if *just now* He had borne our sins in His own body on the Tree, as if *just now* He had said, 'It is finished,' and the soldier had pierced His side and there had come forth blood and water. He is evermore **freshly-slain**."

ii. "This is evidently an allusion to the blood of the victim *newly shed, uncoagulated*, and consequently proper to be use for *sprinkling*. The blood of the Jewish victims was fit for sacrificial purposes only so long as it was *warm and fluid*." (Clarke)

iii. It is a **living way**. Under the Old Covenant, the High Priest had access because of the blood of a dead animal. Now under the New Covenant we have access because of the perfect sacrifice of the sinless Son of God, and it is as if the living, resurrected Jesus ushers us into the throne room of God.

c. **Through the veil**: The **veil** separated **the Holiest** from the *holy place*. To enter into **the Holiest**, you had to pass **through the veil**. But this veil separating man from God's intimate presence is forever opened wide, being torn into two from top to bottom. (Matthew 27:51)

i. **That is, His flesh**: The writer to the Hebrews makes an analogy between the veil that stood between God and man and the body of

Jesus. Jesus' body was "torn," and so was the veil, each indicating that now we can come to God boldly.

ii. "For believers the veil is not rolled up, but rent. The veil was not unhooked, and carefully folded up, and put away, so that it might be put in its place at some future time. Oh, no! But the divine hand took it and rent it front top to bottom. It can never be hung up again; that is impossible. Between those who are in Christ Jesus and the great God, there will never be another separation." (Spurgeon)

iii. "What he does seem to suggest is that it was only when the body of Jesus was torn asunder on the Cross that His life-blood became available for its supreme purpose, the salvation of men." (Robinson)

d. **Having a High Priest over the house of God**: We have a High Priest who presides over the heavenly courts to make certain the believer has total access.

i. "The combination of the **way** and the **Priest** gives us confidence, frees us from fear and all other inhibitions, and makes it possible for us to come, as ourselves, into the presence of God." (Robinson)

ii. "The 'house of God' over which He exercises His high priesthood is, of course, the community of God's people." (Bruce)

2. (22) In light of what Jesus did, let us draw near to God.

Let us draw near with a true heart in full assurance of faith, having our hearts sprinkled from an evil conscience and our bodies washed with pure water.

a. **Let us draw near**: With the perfect cleansing available to us, described in terms of promises of the New Covenant in the Hebrew Scriptures (**hearts sprinkled**) and the Christian practice of baptism (**bodies washed**), we can **draw near** to God in a way never available to someone under the Old Covenant. The work of Jesus makes us able to draw near in a **full assurance of faith**.

i. "Therefore the appeal to me is not a call to prepare myself, or to make a way for myself to God. It is simply to come, to draw near, to enter in. This I do through my great High Priest, but this I may do through Him without faltering and without fear." (Morgan)

ii. **Bodies washed**: "The thing that distinguished Christian baptism from the multiplicity of lustrations that were practiced in the religions of the ancient world was that it was more than an outward rite cleansing the body from ritual defilement. Baptism is the outward sign of an

inward cleansing, and it was the latter that was the more important."
(Morris)

iii. **Hearts sprinkled... bodies washed**: "These participles express not
conditions of approach to God which are not yet to be achieved, but
conditions already possessed." (Dods)

b. **Let us draw near**: We can **draw near** because several issues are settled.
The problem of access to God has been settled. The problem of a perfect
High Priest has been settled. The problem of moral and spiritual pollution
has been settled.

i. The encouragement to **draw near** wouldn't be given unless it was
necessary. These discouraged Christians had a problem in drawing
near. This was their *real* problem: they lost their intimate relationship
with Jesus, and nothing else is going right.

ii. They may have thought that they had many, many problems -
persecution, difficult relationships, hard times with culture or economy.
But the real problem was their relationship with God wasn't on track.
They didn't draw near to God on the basis of what Jesus had done.

iii. When we are in tough times, we should remember that many
people have gone through worse times and have had a better attitude,
and more joy, than you do now. What is the difference? They knew
how to **draw near**.

iv. Just as importantly, the original readers of this letter are reminded
that they will never regain that close relationship with God coming
through the institutions of the Old Covenant.

3. (23) In light of what Jesus did, let us hold fast to the truth.

**Let us hold fast the confession of *our* hope without wavering, for He
who promised *is* faithful.**

a. **Let us hold fast the confession of our hope without wavering**:
Discouragement made them waver from the truth. A renewed confidence
in the greatness of Jesus and in the New Covenant will make them stand
strong in the faith.

i. "That exhortation, 'Let us hold fast,' might well be written on the
cover of every Christian's Bible. We live in such a changeful age, that
we need all to be exhorted to be rooted and grounded, confirmed and
established, in the truth." (Spurgeon)

ii. **Without wavering**: "The Greek word translated in this way is used
only here in the New Testament and is based on the idea of an upright
object not inclining at all from the true perpendicular. There is not

place in the Christian experience for a hope that is firm at one time and shaky at another." (Guthrie)

b. **For He who promised is faithful**: The reason we can stand strong is because **He who promised is faithful**. It is far better to trust in His faithfulness instead of ours!

4. (24-25) In light of what Jesus did, let us pursue the community of God's people.

And let us consider one another in order to stir up love and good works, not forsaking the assembling of ourselves together, as *is* the manner of some, but exhorting *one another*, and so much the more as you see the Day approaching.

a. **Let us consider one another**: Discouragement made them avoid community at the very time they needed it most. Jesus meets us in one another to **stir up love and good works**.

i. **One another**: "The is the only place where the author uses the expression 'one another' (*allelous*), though it is frequently found in the NT. He is speaking of a mutual activity, one in which believers encourage one another, not one where leaders direct the rest as to what they are to do." (Morris)

ii. The wording of **stir up** is strong. "A striking term meaning 'incitement' and is either used, as here, in a good sense or, as in Acts 15:39, in a bad sense (*i.e.* contention). It seems to suggest that loving one another will not just happen." (Guthrie)

iii. **Love** here is the ancient Greek word *agape*, filled with significance by the New Testament. "**Love** needs stimulation and society. **Faith** and **hope** can be practiced by a solitary, in a hermit's cell or on a desert island. But the exercise of **love** is possible only in a community." (Robinson)

b. **Forsaking the assembling of ourselves together**: Forsaking fellowship is a sure way to give place to discouragement. This discouragement festers where God's people are not **exhorting one another**.

i. Some only go to church if they feel they "need it" at the time. But our motivation for fellowship must be to obey God and *to give to others*. We can and should gather with believers to encourage someone who needs to stand strong against a tide of discouragement.

- We gather to receive something from God.
- We gather to give something to God.

- We gather to encourage each other by our shared faith and values.
- We gather to bless one another.
- We gather to work together.

ii. "Any early Christian who attempted to live like a pious particle without the support of the community ran serious risks in an age when there was no public opinion to support him." (Moffatt, cited in Morris) (Morris)

iii. Because it is so important that Christians gather together, things that work *against* their gathering must be regarded as serious dangers. "Schism is the very putting asunder of the very veins and arteries of the mystical body of Christ. We may not separate, but in the sense of intolerable persecution, heresy, idolatry, and Antichristiansim." (Trapp)

iv. "Dr. Mackintosh has well pointed out that the word saint never occurs in the singular, and that 'inevitably it is plural.'" (Thomas)

v. **Assembling**: "The words, *not neglecting to meet together*, presumably refer to worship meetings, although this is not stated. It may purposely be left ambiguous so as to include other gatherings of a more informal kind, but the Greek word (*episynagoge*) suggests some official assembly." (Guthrie)

c. **So much the more as you see the Day approaching**: As **the Day** of Jesus' return draws nearer, we should be *more* committed to the fellowship of God's people, the **assembling of ourselves together**.

i. **As you see the Day approaching**: "It is worth noting in the present context that the verb is indicative and records an accomplished reality - *you see* - and is not as the preceding verbs, in the form of an exhortation. The immanence of the day was considered to be plain. It is not to be regarded as secret. Christians were to live as if the dawning of the day was so near that its arrival was only just beyond the horizon." (Guthrie)

ii. "Each successive Christian generation is called upon to live as the generation of the end-time, if it is to live as a *Christian* generation." (Bruce)

C. Another warning to endure.

1. (26-31) The danger of a willful rejection of Jesus' perfect sacrifice for us.

For if we sin willfully after we have received the knowledge of the truth, there no longer remains a sacrifice for sins, but a certain fearful expectation of judgment, and fiery indignation which will devour the

adversaries. **Anyone who has rejected Moses' law dies without mercy on the testimony of two or three witnesses. Of how much worse punishment, do you suppose, will he be thought worthy who has trampled the Son of God underfoot, counted the blood of the covenant by which he was sanctified a common thing, and insulted the Spirit of grace? For we know Him who said, "Vengeance is Mine, I will repay," says the Lord. And again, "The LORD will judge His people." It is a fearful thing to fall into the hands of the living God.**

a. **For if we sin willfully**: To **sin willfully** is defined in Hebrews 10:29. It speaks of someone who has **trampled the Son of God underfoot, counted the blood of the covenant by which he was sanctified a common thing, and insulted the Spirit of grace**. It is a knowing, deliberate rejection of Jesus' great work for us on the cross.

i. **Sin willfully**: In a sense, *every* sin is a "willful sin." But here, the writer to the Hebrews spoke of something much more severe and relevant to these discouraged Jewish Christians who contemplated a retreat from a distinctive Christianity and a return to Judaism with its sacrificial system. This is turning your back on Jesus.

ii. "It has nothing to do with *backsliders* in our common use of that term. A man may be overtaken in a fault, or he may deliberately go into sin, and yet neither renounce the Gospel, nor deny the Lord that bought him. His case is dreary and dangerous, but it is not *hopeless*." (Clarke)

iii. "The thought seems to be closely connected with the preceding verse, suggesting that if we forsake our fellow-Christians, it may easily lead to our forsaking Christ." (Thomas)

b. **There no longer remains a sacrifice for sins**: If *Jesus'* sacrifice for sin is rejected, there remains *no other* sacrifice that can cleanse.

i. "If this great way of salvation, this mightiest sacrifice of all is refused, no other sacrifice remains." (Morgan)

c. **How much worse punishment**: If someone *does* reject Jesus' sacrifice, fearful judgment is **certain**, even more certain than it was under the Old Covenant.

d. **If we sin willfully after we have received the knowledge of the truth**: When we **sin willfully** by rejecting Jesus' work on the cross as sufficient, we have:

i. **Trampled the Son of God underfoot**: We disgrace Him by rejecting His greatest work. We devalue Him by devaluing what He did. Of this phrase, Vincent notes: "Frequent in LXX for *spoiling, defeating,* *treating contemptuously.* The strong term is purposely selected in order to convey the sense of the fearful outrage involved in forsaking Christ and returning to Judaism."

ii. **Counted the blood of the covenant... a common thing**: We consider Jesus' blood of no greater importance than the countless animals sacrificed under the Old Covenant. Vincent: "Here the word admits of two explanations: (1) that Christ's blood was counted *common*, having no more sacred character or specific worth than the blood of any ordinary person; (2) that in refusing to regard Christ's blood as that of an atoner and redeemer, it was implied that his blood was *unclean* as being that of a transgressor."

iii. **Insulted the Spirit of grace**: We offend the Holy Spirit, whose purpose it is to present Jesus and His work to us (John 16:8-15) when we reject Jesus and His finished work on our behalf.

iv. **Vengeance**: "An unfortunate translation, since it conveys the idea of *vindictiveness* which does not reside in the Greek word. It is the full meting out of justice to all parties." (Vincent)

e. **It is a fearful thing to fall into the hands of the living God**: It is **fearful** indeed to one-day face the God you have rejected and offended so greatly.

i. "To **fall into the hands of the Living God** is, therefore, to have resisted His love, refused His salvation, despised the warnings of His Spirit, and to have persisted thus past the point where God can consistently show further grace." (Newell)

2. (32-34) Take heart in your discouragement, and remember how you have stood for God in tough times before.

But recall the former days in which, after you were illuminated, you endured a great struggle with sufferings: partly while you were made a spectacle both by reproaches and tribulations, and partly while you became companions of those who were so treated; for you had compassion on me in my chains, and joyfully accepted the plundering of your goods, knowing that you have a better and an enduring possession for yourselves in heaven.

a. **But recall the former days**: These Christians had already suffered for Jesus, being rejected from their Jewish community and perhaps being counted as dead. This came after they trusted in Jesus (**after you were illuminated**).

b. **A great struggle with sufferings**: Their persecution was a **struggle** that came many different ways. They were **made a spectacle both by reproaches and tribulations**. They were **companions of those who were so treated**

- including the writer to the Hebrews himself (**you had compassion on me in chains**). They also had faced economic persecution (**the plundering of your goods**). But the point is that they had faced these things, and had **endured** them. They could take a look at their past endurance, and be encouraged to keep standing strong in the future.

> i. Clarke on **a great struggle with sufferings**: "Here we have an allusion to the combats at the Grecian games, or to the exhibitions of gladiators at the public spectacles."

> ii. **Made a spectacle**: This uses the same ancient Greek word as in 1 Corinthians 4:9: *For we have been made a spectacle to the world, both to angels and to men.* The idea is to be made *theater* for a watching world. "Greek, set upon a theatre; take it either properly, or metaphorically, both befell Christians." (Trapp)

c. **Knowing that you have a better and an enduring possession for yourselves in heaven**: They made it through the time of persecution by keeping a heavenly perspective. The writer to the Hebrews' point is clear: you can make it through *this* present time of discouragement also.

3. (35-39) Draw on your past experience to gain strength to endure for the future.

Therefore do not cast away your confidence, which has great reward. For you have need of endurance, so that after you have done the will of God, you may receive the promise:

"For yet a little while,
And **He who is coming will come and will not tarry.**
Now the just shall live by faith;
But if *anyone* **draws back,**
My soul has no pleasure in him."

But we are not of those who draw back to perdition, but of those who believe to the saving of the soul.

a. **Therefore do not cast away your confidence**: These discouraged Christians were in danger of casting **away their confidence** in Jesus, and relapsing into an Old Covenant relationship with God.

> i. **Do not cast away your confidence**: "*Do not throw it away*, μη αποβαλητε, neither men nor devils can take it from you, and God will never deprive you of it if you continue faithful. There is a reference here to cowardly soldiers, who throw away their shields, and run away from the battle. This is your shield, your faith in Christ, which gives you the *knowledge of salvation*; keep it, and it will keep you." (Clarke)

b. **You have need of endurance**: They, and we, **have need of endurance** to receive the promise of God after we **have done the will of God**. The toughest and most discouraging trials are when we are called to obey God's will when the fulfillment of His promise seems so far away. This is why we need **endurance**. Faithfulness during the time when the promise seems unfulfilled is the measure of your obedience and spiritual maturity.

i. This **endurance** is built through trials, the testing of our faith (James 1:2-4).

c. **Now the just shall live by faith**: We need to follow in the footsteps of the **just** who will **live by faith**, and endure to see the promise fulfilled.

i. Every word in Habakkuk 2:4 is important, and the Lord quotes it three times in the New Testament just to bring out the fullness of the meaning.

- In Romans 1:17 Paul quotes this same passage from Habakkuk 2:4 with the emphasis on *faith*: "The just shall live by **faith**."

- In Galatians 3:11 Paul quotes this passage from Habakkuk 2:4 with the emphasis on *just*: "The **just** shall live by faith."

- Here in Hebrews 10:38 the emphasis is on *live*: "The just shall **live** by faith."

d. **But we are not of those who draw back to perdition, but of those who believe to the saving of the soul**: This is a confident conclusion. We *will* be those who endure on and gain the promise of God. We will not **draw back** into old traditions or into an Old Covenant relationship with God - or any other replacement for Jesus.

i. "Drawing back in the Christian life is sometimes due to disappointment, at other times to depression, at still others to discouragement, but always to distrust." (Thomas)

ii. **To the saving of the soul**: "Greek, to the giving of the soul. A metaphor from merchants, who either get more or lose what they have; or else haply from gamesters, who keep stake in store, however the world go with them." (Trapp)

iii. **To the saving of the soul**: "The word 'saving' does not refer to what is generally understood as salvation from sin, but is a word meaning 'complete possession.' Faith is first receptive in spreading its sails to catch the breeze of God's revelation, and then it is responsive to His Word and grace." (Thomas)

Hebrews 11 - Examples of Faith to Help the Discouraged

A. Faith defined.

1. (1) A definition of faith.

Now faith is the substance of things hoped for, the evidence of things not seen.

a. **Now faith is the substance**: Just as our physical eyesight is the sense that gives us evidence of the material world, **faith** is the "sense" that gives us evidence of the invisible, spiritual world.

i. Faith has its reasons. The Bible doesn't recommend a "blind leap" of faith. But the reasons can't be measured in a laboratory; they have to be understood *spiritually*.

ii. "Faith extends beyond what we learn from our senses, and the author is saying that it has its reasons. Its tests are not those of the senses, which yield uncertainty." (Morris)

iii. "Physical eyesight produces a conviction or evidence of visible things; faith is the organ which enables people to see the invisible order." (Bruce)

b. **Of things hoped for... of things not seen**: If you have the substance before you or if you can see it, there is no use for **faith**. Faith is needed for what we *can't* see and *can't* touch.

i. Faith does not contradict reason, though it may go beyond reason. One may objectively prove the Bible is the most unique book ever published and has impacted society more than any other book. But only faith can *prove* that the Bible is the *Word of God*. Therefore, this is a belief *beyond* reason but not in *contradiction* to reason or *against* reason.

c. **Faith is the substance... the evidence**: Faith is *not* a bare belief or intellectual understanding. It is a willingness to trust in, to rely on, and to cling to.

2. (2) Faith enabled people in the past to overcome.

For by it the elders obtained a *good* testimony.

a. **For by it the elders**: The great examples of godliness all had different circumstances and personalities, but they all had one thing in common - faith.

b. **Obtained a good testimony**: These Jewish Christians were discouraged and thought of giving up on Jesus and a distinctive Christianity. They needed **a good testimony**, and so they needed these examples of faith to break them out of discouragement.

3. (3) Faith gives understanding regarding the invisible world.

By faith we understand that the worlds were framed by the word of God, so that the things which are seen were not made of things which are visible.

a. **By faith we understand that the worlds were framed by the word**: This happened when God simply commanded, *"Let there be light"* (Genesis 1:3). As the Psalmist explained: *By the word of the LORD the heavens were made, and all the host of them by the breath of His mouth... For He spoke, and it was done; He commanded, and it stood fast."* (Psalm 33:6, 33:9)

b. **By faith we understand**: We did not see this act of creation; we only know of it by **faith**. We also know this by *reason*, because we know the world was created and created by an intelligent Designer. Again, this is faith going *beyond* but not in *contradiction* to reason.

i. Even in times when it seems when God expects a faith that contradicts reason, closer examination reveals He does not. For example, it might seem contrary to reason for God to expect Abraham to believe that Sarah's dead womb could bring forth a child. But it is not unreasonable to believe that the God who created life and the womb could do this, and that He would do it according to His promise.

c. **By faith we understand**: This text *does not* say that God created the world *with* or *by* **faith**. Since God sees and knows all things, "faith" in a human sense does not apply to Him. Since we understand faith as *the substance of things hoped for, the evidence of things not seen*, what know that God sees everything and does not "hope" for anything.

d. **So that the things which are seen were not made of things which are visible**: Most scientists at the time the Book of Hebrews was written believed the universe was created out of existing matter, not out of nothing. They believed the world was made out of **things which are visible**. But the Bible corrects this misunderstanding, clearly saying that the world was **not made of things which are visible**.

B. Faith at the beginning of man's history.

1. (4) Abel's faith.

By faith Abel offered to God a more excellent sacrifice than Cain, through which he obtained witness that he was righteous, God testifying of his gifts; and through it he being dead still speaks.

a. **By faith Abel offered to God a more excellent sacrifice**: The difference between the sacrifice of Cain and the sacrifice of Abel (Genesis 4:3-5) was not between animal and vegetable. The difference was that Abel's sacrifice was made **by faith**.

i. "Abel's sacrifice was preferred to his brother's for no other reason than that it was sanctified by faith; for surely the fat of brute animals did not smell so sweetly, that it could, by its odour, pacify God." (Calvin)

b. **God testifying of his gifts**: It is likely that God testified of His pleasure with Abel's sacrifice by consuming it with fire from heaven, as happened at the dedication of tabernacle (Leviticus 9:24), the temple (2 Chronicles 7:1) and upon offerings made by David (1 Chronicles 21:26) and Elijah (1 Kings 18:38).

c. **Through it he being dead still speaks**: Right off with his example of Abel, the writer reminds us that faith is not necessarily rewarded on earth. But God Himself testifies to the righteousness of the faithful. Abel's blood still speaks to us, reminding us of the value of eternity.

2. (5-6) Enoch's faith.

By faith Enoch was taken away so that he did not see death, "and was not found, because God had taken him"; for before he was taken he had this testimony, that he pleased God. But without faith *it is* impossible to please *Him*, for he who comes to God must believe that He is, and *that* He is a rewarder of those who diligently seek Him.

a. **By faith Enoch**: Enoch is one of the mystery men of the Old Testament being mentioned only in Genesis 5:21-24 as the man who *walked with God and he was not, for God took him.*

i. Many Jewish and Christian traditions make Enoch the recipient of some spectacular and strange revelations. Jude recognized him as a prophet (Jude 14-15). But the value of other prophecies attributed to him is uncertain at the very best.

b. **By faith Enoch was taken away so that he did not see death**: The writer to the Hebrews assumed that only a man of faith could enjoy close communion with God. Obviously, anyone who had this kind of fellowship with God must have pleased God, and in pleasing God, Enoch fulfilled the purpose for which man was created (Revelation 4:11).

c. **But without faith it is impossible to please Him**: This is the basic faith required of any who seeks God. One must **believe that He is**, and one must believe **He is a rewarder of those who diligently seek Him**. We must believe that God is there, and that He will reveal Himself to the seeking heart.

> i. The writer to the Hebrews didn't say that it is *difficult* to please God without faith. He said that it is **impossible**.

> ii. "These two elements seem most simple, but, alas, how many professing Christians act as if God were not living; and how many others, though seeking after Him, are not *expecting from Him* as Rewarder!" (Newell)

3. (7) Noah's faith.

By faith Noah, being divinely warned of things not yet seen, moved with godly fear, prepared an ark for the saving of his household, by which he condemned the world and became heir of the righteousness which is according to faith.

a. **Noah, being divinely warned of things not yet seen**: Noah was warned of something that had never happened before. His faith was shown in not merely agreeing that the flood would come, but in doing what God told him to do regarding the flood - he was **moved with godly fear**.

b. **Prepared an ark**: Real faith will always *do* something. The book of James repeats this theme over and over again.

c. **He condemned the world**: We shouldn't think that Noah was a man who preached sermons of condemnation to the world. Instead, the mere conduct of the godly, without any preaching at all, can feel like condemnation to the world.

C. Faith in the life of Abraham and the Patriarchs.

1. (8) Abraham's obedience by faith.

By faith Abraham obeyed when he was called to go out to the place which he would receive as an inheritance. And he went out, not knowing where he was going.

a. **By faith, Abraham obeyed**: Abraham did step out in faith, going to the place God promised him; but his faith was less than perfect. This is seen by comparing Genesis 12:1-5 with Acts 7:2-4, where it is evident that Abraham first went half way to where God called him, and only *eventually* obeyed completely. Yet thousands of years later, God did not "remember" the delayed obedience, only the faith.

2. (9-10) Abraham's sojourning life of faith.

By faith he dwelt in the land of promise as *in* a foreign country, dwelling in tents with Isaac and Jacob, the heirs with him of the same promise; for he waited for the city which has foundations, whose builder and maker *is* God.

a. **By faith, he dwelt in the land of promise**: Abraham lived as a "sojourner" in the land God promised, never owning any of it except the plots that he and Sarah were buried on. **Dwelt** translates the ancient Greek word *paroikos*, describing a "resident alien" - one who lives at a certain place, but doesn't have permanent status there.

i. A resident alien or a sojourner is evident. The way they talk, the way they dress, their mannerisms, their entertainment, their citizenship, and their friends, all speak of their native home. If someone is the same in all these areas as the "natives," they are no longer sojourners - they are permanent residents. Christians shouldn't live as if they were permanent residents of planet earth.

b. **Dwelling in tents with Isaac and Jacob**: Because they had no permanent home, Abraham, Isaac and Jacob lived in **tents** instead of houses. They looked forward to a better city - **the city which has foundations, who builder and maker is God**.

3. (11-12) Sarah's faith and its results.

By faith Sarah herself also received strength to conceive seed, and she bore a child when she was past the age, because she judged Him faithful who had promised. Therefore from one man, and him as good as dead, were born *as many* as the stars of the sky in multitude; innumerable as the sand which is by the seashore.

a. **By faith Sarah**: Sarah's faith was not perfect. She first laughed in unbelief (Genesis 18:9-15) and then she learned to laugh in faith (Genesis 21:6).

b. **Because she judged Him faithful who had promised**: Faith comes down to judging that God is faithful and able to keep His promises. It was this faith that enabled Sarah to **receive strength to conceive seed**. God gave the strength, but Sarah received it by faith.

c. **Were born as many as the stars of the sky in multitude**: Because of the faith of Sarah and Abraham, thousands - even millions - of descendants were born. Their faith had impacted more lives than they ever dreamed of.

4. (13-16) What the faith of Abraham and Sarah teaches us.

These all died in faith, not having received the promises, but having seen them afar off were assured of them, embraced *them* and confessed that they were strangers and pilgrims on the earth. For those who say such things declare plainly that they seek a homeland. And truly if they had called to mind that *country* from which they had come out, they would have had opportunity to return. But now they desire a better, that is, a heavenly *country*. Therefore God is not ashamed to be called their God, for He has prepared a city for them.

a. **These all died in faith, not having received the promises**: The promise of the Messiah was made to Abraham and Sarah, and they believed the promise. Yet they **died** having never received it, only seeing it **in faith**.

i. They **saw the promises afar off**, willing to look at and consider the promise of God, even though the fulfillment seemed so far away.

ii. They **were assured of them**, carefully considering the promise, assured that the promise was valid because *God* made the promise.

iii. They **embraced them**, taking the promise and embracing it in faith. Abraham and Sarah probably thought many times a day about the son God promised them and these many times they **embraced** the promise. "*The saints 'embraced' the promises*. The Greek word signifies 'salutes,' as when we see a friend at a distance." (Spurgeon)

iv. They **confessed that they were strangers and pilgrims**: Abraham and Sarah always took the promise with the understanding that this world was not their home. They knew God had a better and more enduring home for them in heaven.

v. If these examples of faith endured through difficulty and discouragement without **having received the promises**, then we who *have* received the promises have even more reason for endurance.

iv. **These all died in faith**:

- They did not need to seek faith on their deathbed. They **died in faith**.

- Though they did have faith, they did also die. We do not have faith to escape death, but to die **in faith**.

- They never went *beyond* faith and "grew beyond" simple dependence on God.

- They never went *below* faith or lost faith.

b. **They seek a homeland... they desire a better, that is, a heavenly country**: Living by faith is easier when we remember that this world is not our home. It is easier when we remember that on this side of eternity, not everything is settled and not every wrong is righted. That is why they **seek a homeland** and a **better... heavenly country**.

i. Faith is very difficult when we live as "practical atheists." This describes someone who may have a theoretical belief in God, but the belief doesn't *matter* in what they do from day to day. When we remember there is a spiritual reality - a heavenly home that is our real home - faith is much easier.

ii. The great theme of modern times is *naturalism*, the belief that only what can be found and measured in nature is "real." Scientists and educators who trust in naturalism may be content to let us believe in God, just as long as we agree that God is a fairy tale - someone not *real*. But when we believe in the *reality* of God and of heaven and of His word, it is completely unacceptable to those who live by naturalism.

iii. H.L. Mencken said faith is the "Illogical belief in the occurrence of the impossible." This would only be true if there is no God or if He does not matter. Since God *is* and since He *does* matter, faith is entirely logical.

c. **Therefore God is not ashamed to be called their God**: For those courageous enough to believe in God, and to believe in Him as *real*, and heaven and eternal life as *real*, **God is not ashamed to be called their God, for He has prepared a city for them**.

i. We often consider the idea that we should not be ashamed of God, but we must also consider that we may make God ashamed of us. When we do not regard God and heaven and eternity as real, there can be a sense in which God is **ashamed to be called our God**.

5. (17-19) Abraham's faith was great enough to know God was able to raise the dead, and that God was able to keep His promises.

By faith Abraham, when he was tested, offered up Isaac, and he who had received the promises offered up his only begotten *son*, of whom it was said, "In Isaac your seed shall be called," concluding that God *was* able to raise *him* up, even from the dead, from which he also received him in a figurative sense.

a. **By faith Abraham, when he was tested, offered up Isaac**: The verb tense for **offered up** indicates that as far as Abraham was concerned the sacrifice was complete. In his will and in his purpose he really did sacrifice his son.

b. **Offered up his only begotten son**: Though Abraham had another son (Ishmael, the son of his fleshly attempt to fulfill God's promise), God did not recognize the other son (Genesis 22:1-14) - so Isaac could be called **his only begotten son**.

c. **Accounting that God was able**: The ancient Greek word translated **accounting** means just what it sounds like in English. It is a term from arithmetic expressing "a decisive and carefully reasoned act." (Guthrie) This means that Abraham calculated God's promise worthy of confidence.

d. **From the dead, from which he also received him**: As far as Abraham was concerned, Isaac was as good as dead and it was from the dead that he received him back, in a manner that prefigured the resurrection of Jesus.

i. Bruce wonders if this is not the incident that Jesus referred to in John 8:56 when Jesus said: *Your father Abraham rejoiced to see My day; and he saw it, and was glad.*

ii. When Abraham was confronted with a promise and a command from God which seemed to contradict each other, he did what we all should do: he obeyed the command and let God take care of the promise. God was more than able to do this.

6. (20) Isaac's faith.

By faith Isaac blessed Jacob and Esau concerning things to come.

a. **By faith Isaac blessed Jacob**: Isaac was really in the *flesh*, not in **faith**, when he first intended to bless Esau instead of Jacob. He wanted to bless Esau with the birthright for carnal reasons. He liked Esau as a more "manly" man, and he liked the wild game he brought home. Instead he should have chosen Jacob, whom God chose.

b. **By faith Isaac blessed**: Yet Isaac came to the place of **faith** when he discovered that he had actually blessed Jacob instead of Esau. Genesis 27:33 says, *Isaac trembled exceedingly.* When *Isaac trembled exceedingly*, he was troubled because he knew that he had tried to box God in, to defeat God's plan, and that God beat him. He realized that he would always be defeated when he tried to resist God's will, even when he didn't like it. And he came to learn that despite his arrogant attempts against the will of God, God's will was glorious.

c. **By faith**: The **faith** in Isaac's blessing came in after Isaac's attempt to thwart the will of God was destroyed, when he said of Jacob, *and indeed he shall be blessed* (Genesis 27:33). He knew that his puny attempt to box God in was defeated, and he responded in the faith that said, "O.K. God, You win. Let Isaac be blessed with the birthright, and let Esau be blessed after him in his own way."

7. (21) Jacob's faith.

By faith Jacob, when he was dying, blessed each of the sons of Joseph, and worshiped, *leaning* on the top of his staff.

a. **By faith Jacob, when he was dying, blessed each of the sons of Joseph**: Jacob led a rather carnal life. Yet his faith could also look beyond death - and he blessed each of his sons.

b. **And worshipped, leaning on the top of his staff**: Jacob had to lean **on the top of his staff** because he was given a limp many years before when God confronted him at Peniel (Genesis 32:24-32). As he leaned on his staff he remembered that God was great and held his future and the future of his descendants. Therefore he **worshiped**, demonstrating his faith and dependence on God.

8. (22) Joseph's faith.

By faith Joseph, when he was dying, made mention of the departure of the children of Israel, and gave instructions concerning his bones.

a. **By faith Joseph**: Joseph **made mention of the departure of the children of Israel** in Genesis 50:24, when he said: *God will surely visit you, and bring you out of this land to the land of which He swore to Abraham, to Isaac, and to Jacob.* He knew God's promise was true!

b. **Gave instructions concerning his bones**: When Joseph died he was never buried. His coffin laid above ground for the 400 or so years until it was taken back to Canaan. It was a silent witness all those years that Israel *was* going back to the Promised Land, just as God had said.

i. "The Holy Spirit in this chapter selects out of good men's lives the most brilliant instances of their faith. I should hardly have expected that he would have mentioned the dying scene of Joseph's life as the most illustrious proof of his faith in God... Does not this tell us, dear brethren and sisters, that we are very poor judges of what God will most delight in?" (Spurgeon)

c. **By faith Joseph**: Joseph's faith testified for years after his death. All during that time, when a child of Israel saw Joseph's coffin and asked why it was there and not buried, they could be answered, "Because the great man Joseph did not want to be buried in Egypt, but in the Promised Land God will one day lead us to."

D. Faith in the nation of Israel.

1. (23) The faith of Moses' parents.

By faith Moses, when he was born, was hidden three months by his parents, because they saw *he was* a beautiful child; and they were not afraid of the king's command.

a. **By faith Moses... was hidden three months by his parents**: Moses' parents showed faith when they perceived that he was specially favored by God they took measures of faith to save his life despite danger.

b. **They were not afraid of the king's command**: When the Pharaoh of Egypt commanded the murder of Hebrew children **faith** gave Moses' parents the courage to obey God instead of man.

2. (24-26) The faith of Moses in Pharaoh's court.

By faith Moses, when he became of age, refused to be called the son of Pharaoh's daughter, choosing rather to suffer affliction with the people of God than to enjoy the passing pleasures of sin, esteeming the reproach of Christ greater riches than the treasures in Egypt; for he looked to the reward.

a. **Refused to be called the son of Pharaoh's daughter**: Moses showed faith when he let God chart his destiny instead of allowing Pharaoh or raw ambition to do it.

b. **Choosing rather to suffer affliction**: This choice had consequences. Moses knew that to go God's way meant to **suffer affliction** rather than **to enjoy the passing pleasures of sin**. Sin does have its pleasures; but Moses properly saw them as passing, even if they should last our entire *earthly* life.

c. **The reproach of Christ**: Moses probably didn't know it at the time but the persecution he suffered for his choice of serving God and His people put him in the company of Jesus - who suffered to set men free.

3. (27) The faith of Moses when he left Egypt.

By faith he forsook Egypt, not fearing the wrath of the king; for he endured as seeing Him who is invisible.

a. **By faith he forsook Egypt, not fearing the wrath of the king**: Moses' natural eyes could see the danger from Pharaoh, and he understood the danger in remaining anywhere near Egypt. Yet his eye of faith could see **Him who is invisible**, and he understood that God was a greater fact in his situation than an angry Pharaoh was.

4. (28) Moses showed faith when he led Israel in the Passover, in obedience to God's command.

By faith he kept the Passover and the sprinkling of blood, lest he who destroyed the firstborn should touch them.

a. **By faith he kept the Passover**: It took faith to believe that the blood of a lamb on the doorpost would save a household from the terror of the angel of death. But Moses had that faith and led the nation in observing **the Passover**.

b. **Lest he who destroyed the firstborn should touch them**: Those who did not share the **faith** of Moses and obedient Israel found their firstborn sons **destroyed** at that first Passover. They did not trust in the blood of the Passover Lamb.

5. (29) The faith of the nation of Israel when crossing the Red Sea.

By faith they passed through the Red Sea as by dry *land, whereas* the Egyptians, attempting *to do* so, were drowned.

a. **By faith they passed through the Red Sea**: The difference between the Israelites crossing the Red Sea and the Egyptians who followed them was not courage, but faith.

b. **The Egyptians, attempting to do so, were drowned**: The Egyptians had as much (or more) courage than the Israelites, but not the same **faith** - and they each had different fates. The Israelites **passed through** and the Egyptians **were drowned**.

6. (30) The faith of the nation of Israel when circling around Jericho as God had commanded.

By faith the walls of Jericho fell down after they were encircled for seven days.

a. **By faith the walls of Jericho fell down**: At Jericho, the people of Israel had a *daring* faith. There was no turning back, having already crossed the river Jordan at flood stage, which cut off any line of retreat.

b. **After they were encircled for seven days**: At Jericho the people of Israel had an *obedient* faith. They did not really understand what God was doing, yet they obeyed nonetheless.

c. **After they were encircled for seven days**: At Jericho the people of Israel had a *patient* faith. The walls did not fall down for the first six days, yet they kept marching as God commanded.

d. **For seven days**: At Jericho the people of Israel had an *anticipating* faith. They knew God would act on the seventh day when they shouted.

7. (31) The faith of Rahab.

By faith the harlot Rahab did not perish with those who did not believe, when she had received the spies with peace.

a. **By faith the harlot Rahab did not perish**: Joshua 2 tells us of **Rahab**, who might seem an unusual example of faith. Yet her willingness to become a traitor to the gods of Canaan and to identify with Yahweh with His people despite the cost is worthy of praise.

> i. "She was a harlot, a woman that was a sinner, and universally known to be such. Desperate attempts have been made to find some other meaning for the word rendered harlot, but they have been utterly fruitless." (Spurgeon) Spurgeon described Rahab's faith like this:
>
> - Saving faith.
> - Singular faith.
> - Stable faith.
> - Self-denying faith.
> - Sympathizing faith.
> - Sanctifying faith.

b. **When she had received the spies with peace**: When the Hebrew spies came to Rahab, she declared *He is God in heaven above and on earth beneath* (Joshua 2:11). This was proof of her faith. It was not strong faith and it was not perfect faith, but her faith was commendable nonetheless.

> i. Clement of Rome, the earliest Christian writer outside of the Bible, was the first the see a symbol of the blood of Jesus in the scarlet cord that Rahab set outside her window (Joshua 2:18).

8. (32) Other heroes of faith.

And what more shall I say? For the time would fail me to tell of Gideon and Barak and Samson and Jephthah, also *of* David and Samuel and the prophets:

a. **Gideon**: He boldly destroyed idols and was mightily used of God to defeat a much larger army of Midianites (Judges 6-7). Yet he was also a man who doubted God's word to him at first and repeatedly asked for confirmation.

b. **Barak**: He led the people of Israel in a dramatic victory over the Canaanites (Judges 4). Yet he hesitated and went forward only when Deborah encouraged him.

c. **Samson**: He was used mightily of the Lord to defeat the Philistines. Yet he never lived up to his potential, and had a tragic ending to his life after being enticed by Delilah (Judges 13-16).

d. **Jephthah**: He was used of God to defeat the Ammonites. Yet Jephthah made a foolish vow and stubbornly kept it (Judges 11).

e. **David**: The great king of Israel was a remarkable man of faith. Yet he also failed with Bathsheba and with his own children.

i. Each one of these were men of faith, yet had notable areas of failure in their life. Still, Hebrews 11 commends their faith and lists them in the "Hall of Faith." This shows that weak faith is better than unbelief, and you don't have to be perfect to make it into God's "Hall of Faith."

9. (33-35a) By faith, some were victorious *over* circumstances.

Who through faith subdued kingdoms, worked righteousness, obtained promises, stopped the mouths of lions, quenched the violence of fire, escaped the edge of the sword, out of weakness were made strong, became valiant in battle, turned to flight the armies of the aliens. Women received their dead raised to life again.

a. **Subdued kingdoms**: Some of these were David, Joshua, King Asa, Jehoshaphat, King Hezekiah, and King Josiah.

b. **Worked righteousness**: Some of these were Elijah, Elisha, and the other prophets in general; King Josiah also.

c. **Obtained promises**: Among these we could include Caleb, Gideon, and Barak.

d. **Stopped the mouths of lions**: These include Daniel, David, and Benaiah (one of David's mighty men).

d. **Quenched the violence of fire**: Among these are Shadrach, Meshach, and Abednego.

e. **Escaped the edge of the sword**: David escaped the sword of Goliath and the sword of Saul, Moses escaped the sword of Pharaoh, and Elijah escaped the sword of Jezebel.

f. **Out of weakness were made strong**: Among these are Sarah, Gideon, Abraham, Esther, and King Hezekiah.

i. "Many of us may never have to brave the fiery stake, nor to bow our necks upon the block, to die as Paul did; but if we have grace enough to be out of weakness made strong, we shall not be left out of the roll of the nobles of faith, and God's name shall not fail to be glorified in our persons." (Spurgeon)

g. **Became valiant in battle**: Some of the many in this description are David, King Asa, and Jehoshaphat.

h. **Women who received their dead raised to life again**: The Old Testament mentions at least two who fit this description, the widow of Zarepheth and the Shunamite woman.

10. (35b-38) By faith, some were victorious *under* their circumstances.

And others were tortured, not accepting deliverance, that they might obtain a better resurrection. Still others had trial of mockings and scourgings, yes, and of chains and imprisonment. They were stoned, they were sawn in two, were tempted, were slain with the sword. They wandered about in sheepskins and goatskins, being destitute, afflicted, tormented—of whom the world was not worthy. They wandered in deserts and mountains, *in* dens and caves of the earth.

a. **Tortured**: This is a brutal word in the ancient Greek language. It carries the idea "to beat with a stick or a baton."

b. **A better resurrection**: As Jesus said in John 5:29, there is a resurrection unto life *and* a resurrection unto condemnation. These worthies received the **better resurrection**.

c. **Trial of mockings**: Isaac endured the cruel mocking of Ishmael, and Samson was mocked at the feast of the Philistines.

d. **Chains and imprisonments**: Joseph was cast into prison for his faith, and the evil King Ahab imprisoned the prophet Micaiah.

e. **They were stoned**: Zechariah was stoned to death between the altar and the temple and Naboth was stoned to death by Jezebel's henchmen.

f. **Sawn in two**: According to reliable tradition Isaiah was **sawn in two** and killed.

g. **Were tempted**: Among these terrible physical tortures, the writer brings up being **tempted** in the same context. Some think the text was corrupted here and the writer to the Hebrews originally wrote, "branded," "burnt alive," "mutilated," or "strangled." But for those who know the pain of temptation, it is not unreasonable to think that the writer regarded overcoming temptation as a true triumph of faith.

i. "'They were tempted': it does not say how. If one form of temptation had been mentioned, we should have surmised that they did not suffer in other ways, but when the statement is, 'they were tempted,' we shall not be wrong in concluding that they were tried in any and every form." (Spurgeon)

h. **Were slain with the sword**: Such as the eighty-five priests murdered by Doeg, or the prophets murdered in Elijah's day.

i. **Wandered about in sheepskins and goatskins**: Such as Elijah, who wore this kind humble clothing and did not mind the humility or the discomfort.

j. **Of whom the world was not worthy**: The world is not necessarily friendly to people of faith, and the world isn't necessarily **worthy** of them either.

i. "The despised and ill-treated group of servants of God was of greater real worth than all the rest of humanity put together." (Morris)

k. **In dens and caves of the earth**: David, Elijah, and prophets under the leadership of Obadiah were all forced to flee and hide in caves.

11. (39-40) Conclusion: We have even more reasons for faith, more reasons to hold on to faith, than these heroes of the faith did.

And all these, having obtained a good testimony through faith, did not receive the promise, God having provided something better for us, that they should not be made perfect apart from us.

a. **Having obtained a good testimony through faith**: Though they obtained this good testimony, they did not they **did not receive the promise**, the testimony of the completed work of the Messiah on their behalf. If these followers of God were steadfast without receiving the promise, those who have received the promise have even more reason to be continue on through trials and difficulty.

b. **God having provided something better for us**: We are **provided something better** (seeing and enjoying the completed work of Jesus on our behalf) and therefore have *much more reason* to hold on to faith, and to not let discouragement and tough times defeat us.

c. **They should not be made perfect apart from us**: The idea of **perfect** is "complete." They could not be made complete until the work of Jesus. They looked forward to Jesus and His work, we look at it from behind - and enjoy the fruit of His work.

i. "This chapter proves that the saints of all ages are essentially one. There is a link which unites them; a thrill which passes from one hand to hand around the circle." (Meyer)

ii. Their faithfulness makes our faith a little easier. The writer to the Hebrews began this chapter speaking of faith in the *present* tense: *Now faith is... By faith we understand* (Hebrews 11:1 and 11:3). The end of the chapter reminds us that faith *is* and it is for *we* who follow in the footsteps of the faithful men and women of previous ages.

iii. "It is what Christ has done that opens the way into the very presence of God for them as for us. Only the work of Christ brings those of Old Testament times and those of the new and living way alike into the presence of God." (Morris)

Hebrews 12 - Reasons to Endure Discouraging Times

A. Look unto Jesus.

1. (1) Application of the demonstrations of enduring faith in Hebrews 11.

Therefore we also, since we are surrounded by so great a cloud of witnesses, let us lay aside every weight, and the sin which so easily ensnares *us*, and let us run with endurance the race that is set before us,

a. **Since we are surrounded by so great a cloud of witnesses**: In the mind's eye, the author pictured these previous champions of faith as spectators from the heavens, cheering us as we press on to overcome present discouragement as in an athletic competition.

i. The author thought of many more than just the 18 specifically mentioned in Hebrews 11. The ancient Greek word translated **cloud** was a figure of speech indicating a large group, and this is **so great a cloud of witnesses**. That **cloud** probably includes great men and women of God who have come since those Hebrews 11 saints, known and unknown to history. We are also under angelic observation (Ephesians 3:10-11) and the world watches our faith and conduct. We **are surrounded** by them, as spectators in a stadium surround and observe the players.

ii. The idea of the heroes of faith in the past being spectators as we live lives of faith has made some think that in heaven, people can and do observe what goes on earth. This single passage may *suggest* this, but it is inconclusive to *prove* this.

iii. We rightly think of heaven as a place where people are always happy and untroubled. It is hard to think that those in heaven are happy and untroubled if they see what is happening on the earth. So, it is difficult to say that people in heaven are actually observing us.

135

iv. Others consider that these **witnesses** are not witnessing *us* as we conduct our lives. Instead, they are **witnesses** *to* us of faith and endurance, in all they have lived and experienced. They have the spirit of *martyrs* - the root of the ancient Greek word translated **witnesses**.

v. "Both the *Greeks* and the *Latins* frequently use the term *cloud,* to express a *great number* of persons or things." (Clarke)

b. **Let us lay aside every weight, and the sin**: Sin can hold us back. But there are also things that may not be sin (**every weight**) but are merely hindrances that can keep us from running effectively the race God has for us.

i. Our choices are not always between right and wrong, but between something that may hinder us and something else that may not. Is there a **weight** in your life you must **lay aside**?

c. **The sin which so easily ensnares us**: The words **easily ensnares** translate a difficult ancient Greek word (*euperistaton*), which can be translated four ways: "easily avoided," "admired," "ensnaring," or "dangerous."

i. Let us **lay** them *all* **aside**:

- Some sins can be *easily avoided,* but are not.
- Some sins are *admired,* yet must be laid aside.
- Some sins are *ensnaring* and thus especially harmful.
- Some sins are more *dangerous* than others are.

ii. If such ensnaring sins were really the work of demonic possession or demonic influence in the Christian, this would be an ideal place for the Holy Spirit to address this. Yet we are never given reason to blame our sin on demons; the appeal is simply for us to, in the power of the Holy Spirit, **lay aside every weight, and the sin which so easily ensnares us**.

d. **Let us run with endurance**: What is needed is **endurance**, to finish what we have begun in Jesus Christ - a **race that is set before us**.

i. "He stands with us at the starting-point, and earnestly says to us, not 'Run,' but, 'Let us run.' The apostle himself is at our side as a runner." (Spurgeon)

ii. God has set before you - and each of us - a **race**. You must run it, and it will involve effort and commitment. Being passive never runs or wins a race. God wants us to run the race and to finish it right.

iii. **Endurance** is needed to run that race. **Endurance** translates the ancient Greek word *hupomone,* "which does not mean the patience which sits down and accepts things but the patience which masters them... It is a determination, unhurrying and yet undelaying, which goes steadily on and refuses to be deflected." (Barclay)

iv. In Acts 20:24 Paul pictured himself as a runner who had a race to finish, and nothing would keep Paul from finishing the race with joy. In that passage, Paul spoke of *my race* - he had his race to run, we have our own - but God calls us to finish it with joy, and that only happens with **endurance**.

e. **The race that is set before us**: **Race** is the ancient Greek word *agona*, a word used for conflict or struggle of many kinds, and a favorite word of Paul (Philippians 1:30, Colossians 2:1, 1 Thessalonians 2:2, 1 Timothy 6:12, 2 Timothy 4:7).

2. (2) The ultimate example: Jesus Christ.

Looking unto Jesus, the author and finisher of *our* faith, who for the joy that was set before Him endured the cross, despising the shame, and has sat down at the right hand of the throne of God.

a. **Looking unto Jesus**: The *New American Standard Version* translates this beautifully as, *fixing our eyes on Jesus*. We can only run the race as we look to Jesus and have our eyes locked on to Him. He is our focus, our inspiration, and our example.

i. In the ancient Greek, **looking unto Jesus** uses a verb that implies a definite *looking away* from other things and a present *looking unto* Jesus.

ii. "The Greek word for 'looking' is a much fuller word than we can find in the English language. It has a preposition in it which turns the look away from everything else. You are to look from all beside to Jesus. Fix not thy gaze upon the cloud of witnesses; they will hinder thee if they take away thine eye from Jesus. Look not on the weights and the besetting sin-these thou hast laid aside; look away from them. Do not even look upon the race-course, or the competitors, but look to Jesus and so start in the race." (Spurgeon)

iii. We must guard against seeing Jesus as *only* an example; He was and is so much more. But He also remains the ultimate example of Christian endurance. "Looking unto Jesus means life, light, guidance, encouragement, joy: never cease to look on him who ever looks on you." (Spurgeon)

b. **The author and finisher of our faith**: Jesus is not only the **author** of our faith; He is the **finisher** of it also. The idea of *He who has begun a good* *work in you will complete it until the day of Jesus Christ* (Philippians 1:6) was comforting indeed to these discouraged Christians.

i. One may say that Jesus is with us at the starting line and the finish line and all along the way of the race that He sets before us.

c. **Who for the joy that was set before Him**: Jesus did not regard the cross itself as a joy. But He could look past the horror of the cross to enjoy the joy beyond it. The same mentality would enable these Jewish Christians (and we ourselves) to endure.

d. **Endured the cross**: Jesus was able to endure the ordeal of the cross because He understood the *good* that would come of it - the good of a redeemed, rescued people honoring God for all eternity.

i. Knowing all the good that would flow from this most agonizing experience, Jesus was able to do it and to endure it with triumph. Through the ordeal of the cross:

- Jesus kept His tongue.
- Jesus kept His course.
- Jesus kept His progress.
- Jesus kept His joy.
- Jesus kept His love.

e. **Despising the shame**: One of the most prominent elements of the torture of the cross was its extreme **shame**. Jesus did not welcome this shame - He *despised* it - yet He endured through it to victory.

i. Shame is a significant trial. Daniel 12:2 says that shame will be an aspect of the terrors of hell: *And many of those who sleep in the dust of the earth shall awake, some to everlasting life, some to shame and everlasting contempt.* Jesus bore this hellish shame to accomplish our redemption.

- Jesus bore a shameful accusation: blasphemy.
- Jesus bore shameful mocking.
- Jesus bore a shameful beating.
- Jesus wore a shameful crown.
- Jesus wore a shameful robe.
- Jesus bore a shameful mocking even as He prayed on the cross.

ii. This is a stumbling block to many. They will do just about anything for Jesus *except* endure shame or embarrassment. Spurgeon spoke boldly to Christians who could not bear shame comes from the world for following Jesus: "Yet you are a coward. Yes, put it down in English:

you are a coward. If anybody called you so you would turn red in the face; and perhaps you are not a coward in reference to any other subject. What a shameful thing it is that while you are bold about everything else you are cowardly about Jesus Christ. Brave for the world and cowardly towards Christ!"

iii. "I heard of a prayer the other day which I did not quite like at first, but there is something in it after all. The good man said, 'Lord, if our hearts are hard, make them soft; but if our hearts are too soft, make them hard.' I know what he meant, and I think I can pray that last prayer for some of my friends who are so delicate that a sneer would kill them. May the Lord harden them till they can despise the shame!" (Spurgeon)

f. **And has sat down at the right hand of the throne of God**: This speaks of Jesus' glorification. The same promise of being glorified (though in a different sense) after our shame is true for the Christian.

3. (3-4) Consider Jesus.

For consider Him who endured such hostility from sinners against Himself, lest you become weary and discouraged in your souls. You have not yet resisted to bloodshed, striving against sin.

a. **Consider Him who endured such hostility from sinners against Himself**: Even in their difficulty if they would **consider** Jesus they could be *encouraged*, not *discouraged*, knowing that they were following in the footsteps of Jesus. As Paul wrote, *if indeed we suffer with Him, that we may also be glorified together*. (Romans 8:17)

i. Think of all the hostility Jesus endured from sinners:

- At His own synagogue in Nazareth they wanted to kill Him.
- The religious leaders constantly tried to trap and embarrass Him.
- They lied about Jesus, saying He was a drunkard and a glutton.
- He was betrayed by one of His own disciples.
- He was mocked and beaten by many.
- His own people cried out against Him, "Crucify Him!"

ii. "If in the Sunday-school a class seems unmanageable; if the boys cannot be taught; if the girls seem so giddy; if in the little village station the hearers seem, so dull, so inattentive, so careless, and so forgetful; if in any other sphere of labor you do not seem to be appreciated, but to meet with very serious rebuffs, never mind. These are nothing compared with the contradictions which the Saviour endured, and yet swerved he never, and therefore swerve not you." (Spurgeon)

b. **Lest you become weary and discouraged in your souls**: Knowing that Jesus doesn't ask more of us than what He has Himself experienced, and that He knows exactly what we are going through keeps us from becoming **weary and discouraged in your souls**.

c. **You have not yet resisted to bloodshed, striving against sin**: These Jewish Christians were so discouraged because they started to experience significant social and economic persecution (though **not yet** to the shedding of blood).

B. Why God allows difficult times: the chastening of God.

1. (5-6) Remember the exhortation regarding the discipline of the Lord.

And you have forgotten the exhortation which speaks to you as to sons:

"My son, do not despise the chastening of the LORD,
Nor be discouraged when you are rebuked by Him;
For whom the LORD loves He chastens,
And scourges every son whom He receives."

a. **You have forgotten**: One great reason for the discouragement among these Jewish Christians was because they saw no reason why God would allow difficult times to arise. They forgot principles regarding the **chastening of the LORD**.

i. Much difficulty in the Christian life comes from those three words: **you have forgotten**. Perhaps it is some principle we remember in the mind, but **have forgotten** in the heart - and we must remember it again.

ii. In times of trial or stress many Christians forget some of the basics. The seriously wonder if God is still in control or if He still loves them. We must admit that God does *allow* every thing that happens; so He must at least passively approve of it, because He certainly has the power to stop bad things that happen.

iii. Of course, God can *never* be the author of evil. But He does allow others to choose evil, and He can use the evil choice another makes to work out His ultimately good purpose, even if only to demonstrate His justice and righteousness in contrast to evil.

b. **Which speaks to you as sons**: The quotation from Proverbs 3:11-12 reminds us that God's chastening should *never* be taken as a sign of His rejection. It is rather a sign of His treating us as His children.

i. Only the most proud Christian would claim they are never in need of correction from God. No one is above this training.

c. **Do not despise the chastening of the LORD**: When chastening comes it is an offense to God when we **despise** it. **Chastening** is His loving tool of correction and we should receive it gratefully. This is the training we need to run the race we must run with endurance (Hebrews 12:1-2).

i. "I have often heard a father say, 'Boy, if you cry for that you shall have something to cry for by-and-by.' So, if we murmur at a little God gives us something that will make us cry. If we groan for nothing, he will give us something that will make us groan." (Spurgeon)

ii. **Chastening** should not be regarded as the *only* reason God allows difficult times, but it is an important one. For example, we know that God allows difficult times so that we can, at a later time, comfort someone else with the same comfort God shows towards us in our crisis (2 Corinthians 1:3-7).

iii. This is why James recommends a prayer for wisdom in the context of enduring trials (James 1:2-5). We need to know how to react differently when God does different things.

2. (7-8) Chastening is a sign of being a son of God.

If you endure chastening, God deals with you as with sons; for what son is there whom a father does not chasten? But if you are without chastening, of which all have become partakers, then you are illegitimate and not sons.

a. **God deals with you as sons**: A fundamental fact of the believer's relationship with God is that He is to His people as a loving, good father is to a son or daughter. Some have trouble receiving this because they never knew a loving, good human father in their own experience. Yet, even these can still receive the love of God the Father.

i. We all do not know by *experience* what a model father is, but we all know by *intuition* what a good father is. God is that perfect Father, and He gives us that intuition. One feels cheated or disappointed by a *bad* father because they intuitively compare them to our *good* Father in heaven.

b. **God deals with you as sons**: God's correction is never to punish us or make us *pay* for our sins. That was done once and for all at the cross. His correction is motivated *only* by His love, not by His justice; He chastens us without anger.

i. "While he shall never be arraigned before God's bar as a criminal, and punished for his guilt, yet he now stands in a new relationship- that of a child to his parent: and as a son he may be chastised on account of sin." (Spurgeon)

c. **If you are without chastening... you are illegitimate and not sons**: Those who consider themselves beyond God's correction do not appreciate that it is a mark of a true son, and unknowingly associate themselves with **illegitimate** children of God.

i. "When this attitude is realized, then we understand the direct and blessed connection between 'discipleship' and 'discipline.'" (Thomas)

d. **Illegitimate and not sons**: God shows His *wrath* when He ignores our sin, allowing it to pass without correction. His inactivity is never due to ignorance or a lack of initiative, as may be true with a human father.

3. (9-10) God's chastening is superior to that of human fathers.

Furthermore, we have had human fathers who corrected *us,* and we paid *them* respect. Shall we not much more readily be in subjection to the Father of spirits and live? For they indeed for a few days chastened *us* as seemed *best* to them, but He for *our* profit, that *we* may be partakers of His holiness.

a. **We have had human fathers who corrected us, and we paid them respect**: We should be even more submissive and respectful to our Heavenly Father's correction than to an earthly Father's correction.

b. **Shall we not much more readily be in subjection to the Father of Spirits and live?** Therefore, we must never despise God for His chastening, though it is unpleasant at the moment. When we resent it, we consider ourselves virtual equals with God instead of His children.

i. It can be humiliating and bitter to be chastened by an equal, but it isn't the same to be chastened by someone who is legitimately our superior. Resentment at chastening shows how we see God and how we see ourselves.

c. **But He for our profit**: Human fathers, even with the best of intention, can only chasten imperfectly because they lack perfect knowledge. The all-knowing God can chasten us perfectly, with better and more lasting results than even the best earthly father.

i. "Faith sees that in her worst sorrow there is nothing penal; there is not a drop of God's wrath in it; it is all sent in love." (Spurgeon)

4. (11) Look to the *result* of chastening more than the *process* of chastening.

Now no chastening seems to be joyful for the present, but painful; nevertheless, afterward it yields the peaceable fruit of righteousness to those who have been trained by it.

a. **No chastening seems to be joyful for the present**: Trials are trials and chastening is chastening. If it does not hurt or press us, then they do not serve their purpose. We sometimes want trials that are not trials and chastening that is not chastening.

i. Spurgeon observed that in the natural realm we can be led astray by what **seems** to be. The earth does not seem to move, or seem to be round; the sun seems to be larger at sunset, and so on. "Now, if even in natural things *the seeming* is not the truth, and the appearance is very often false, we may rest quite sure that though affliction seemeth to be one thing, it really is not what it seemeth to be." (Spurgeon)

ii. "If affliction *seemed* to be joyous, would it be a chastisement at all? I ask you, would it not be a most *ridiculous* thing if a father should so chasten a child, that the child came down stairs laughing, and smiling, and rejoicing at the flogging. Joyous? Instead of being at all serviceable, would it not be utterly *useless?* What good could a chastisement have done if it was not felt? No smart? Then surely no benefit!" (Spurgeon)

b. **The peaceable fruit of righteousness**: This **fruit** must be evident in the life of the Christian. The reason why many experience one crisis after another in life is because they are either blind to God's chastening or they resist it. They are not **trained by it** and therefore the **peaceable fruit of righteousness** is not evident.

i. **Trained** in the ancient Greek language is a word from the world of athletics. The training of an athlete is marked by some agony and so is our training as God's "spiritual athletes."

ii. God has a purpose for training you. Think of David after a lion attacked when he was just a boy tending the sheep. He could easily despair and ask, "Why did God allow such a terrible thing to happen to me? I barely escaped!" If David could see ahead, he could see God had a giant named Goliath he was destined to face and the battle with the lion prepared him ahead of time. God always has a purpose. We can trust Him.

c. **Afterward it yields the peaceable fruit of righteousness**: God's correction - a spanking from heaven - smarts, but we must look beyond the *process* to the *result*. The result does not come *immediately*, but **afterward**.

i. "Many believers are deeply grieved, because they do not at once feel that they have been profited by their afflictions. Well, you do not expect to see apples or plums on a tree which you have planted but a week. Only little children put their seeds into their flower-garden, and then expect to see them grow into plants in an hour." (Spurgeon)

ii. We notice that in this section on chastening the author never pointed to Jesus as an example. This is because Jesus never needed to be corrected by His Father. Jesus suffered, but not for the sake of correction.

C. Application: Get strong, get right, get bold, and watch out.

1. (12-13) Take encouragement, be strong.

Therefore strengthen the hands which hang down, and the feeble knees, and make straight paths for your feet, so that what is lame may not be *dislocated*, but rather be healed.

a. **Therefore strengthen the hands which hang down**: Almost like a coach or a military officer, the author told his fellow followers of Jesus to take courage and be active. He gave exhaustive *reasons* to be strong in the Lord and to put off discouragement, the time had now come to *do it*.

b. **But rather be healed**: The pictures here (strengthened **hands** and **knees**, "straight-ahead" **feet**) speak of readiness to work and move for Jesus and His kingdom. This readiness is first to go when one surrenders to discouragement.

2. (14-17) Use God's strength to set things right in your manner of living.

Pursue peace with all *people*, and holiness, without which no one will see the Lord: looking carefully lest anyone fall short of the grace of God; lest any root of bitterness springing up cause trouble, and by this many become defiled; lest there *be* any fornicator or profane person like Esau, who for one morsel of food sold his birthright. For you know that afterward, when he wanted to inherit the blessing, he was rejected, for he found no place for repentance, though he sought it diligently with tears.

a. **Pursue peace with all people, and holiness**: This means to walk right with both men (**pursue peace with all men**) and to walk right with God (**and holiness**). Discouragement makes us sloppy and unconcerned with holiness and personal relationships.

i. Regarding holiness, we are told **without which no one will see the Lord**. A lack of holiness is a critical obstacle to a close relationship with God.

ii. "Unholy Christians are the plague of the church. They are spots in our feasts of charity. Like hidden rocks, they are the terror of navigators.

It is hard to steer clear of them: and there is no telling what wrecks they may cause." (Spurgeon)

iii. At the same time "This holiness is a thing of growth. It may be in the soul as the grain of mustard-seed, and yet not developed; it may be in the heart as a wish and a desire, rather than anything that has been fully realized, — a groaning, a panting, a longing, a striving." (Spurgeon)

iv. Spurgeon described four types of people who try to get on without holiness:

- The *Pharisee*: Confident in outward ceremonies instead of true holiness.

- The *moralist*: Feels no need for holiness because his life is so good.

- The *experimentalist*: Their entire Christian life is lived inward, never looking to outward conduct but only to feelings.

- The *opinionist*: Their Christian life is all about believing the right doctrines and is unconcerned about the way one lives.

b. **Lest anyone fall short of the grace of God**: We must live right in regard to **the grace of God**. This means to diligently keep both our self and others from a return to legalism in either outward form or inward attitude that falls short of God's grace, **lest any root of bitterness springing up cause trouble**.

i. "A *bitter root* is a root that bears bitter fruit… So it is possible for the seed of bitterness to be sown in a community and, though nothing is immediately apparent, in due time the inevitable fruit appears." (Morris)

ii. Bitterness corrupts many, rooted in a sense of personal hurt, and many hold on to the bitterness with amazing stubbornness. What they must do is remember the grace of God extended to them, and start extending that grace towards others - loving the undeserving.

iii. William Barclay wrote that the phrase **fall short of the grace of God** might also be translated *failing to keep up with the grace of God*. The idea is that the grace of God is moving on, past the pain and hurt of the past. We should move on also.

c. **Lest there be any fornicator or profane person**: We must get right in regard to our moral conduct. Remember that there are blessings reserved only for the *pure in heart: they shall see God* (Matthew 5:8).

i. Thomas on **profane**: "It comes from the Latin words *pro-fanum*. Outside every fane or temple there was an area of land open to every one, where people gathered, and open place without enclosure. In contrast with this was the sacred enclosure of the temple or 'fane' itself. Esau had not such sacred enclosure in his life, and in this sense was a purely secular man."

d. **Like Esau, who for one morsel of food sold his birthright**: Many Christians today sell a birthright of intimacy with God as cheaply as Esau sold his birthright (Genesis 25:29-34 and 27:30-40).

i. **For he found no place for repentance**: "It is not a question of forgiveness. God's forgiveness is always open to the penitent. Esau could have come back to God. But he could not undo his act." (Morris)

ii. **Though he sought it diligently with tears**: When Esau later sought the blessing **he was rejected** by his father Isaac and **found no place for repentance** before Isaac. Esau's birthright wasn't restored simply because he *wished* it back. It could never be regained because he *despised* it.

3. (18-21) Be bold, because you **have not come** to Mount Sinai.

For you have not come to the mountain that may be touched and that burned with fire, and to blackness and darkness and tempest, and the sound of a trumpet and the voice of words, so that those who heard *it* begged that the word should not be spoken to them anymore. (For they could not endure what was commanded: "And if so much as a beast touches the mountain, it shall be stoned or shot with an arrow." And so terrifying was the sight *that* Moses said, "I am exceedingly afraid and trembling.")

a. **For you have not come to the mountain that may be touched and that burned with fire**: Exodus 19:10-25 explains what it was like when Israel came to Mount Sinai.

- The mountain was fenced off; there was no trespassing on pain of death.

- They were commanded to wash their clothes and abstain from sexual relations.

- There was thunder, lightning and a thick cloud.

- There was the sound of a trumpet, calling forth the nation to meet with God.

- There was more smoke, like a furnace, and earthquakes.

- Then the trumpet sounded long - until Moses spoke, and God Himself answered.

- God spoke to Israel from Sinai, but warned them in every way possible to *stay away*.

b. **So that those who heard it begged that the word should not be spoken to them anymore**: The reaction of Israel was understandable: they were terrified (Exodus 20:18-21). They wanted the experience to *stop*, not to continue.

> i. *Even Moses was afraid*: **Moses said, "I am exceedingly afraid and trembling"** (Deuteronomy 9:19).

> ii. All this fear did not succeed in promoting holiness among the people of Israel. It did not succeed in changing the heart of Israel. 40 days later, they worshipped a gold calf and said it was the god that brought them out of Egypt.

4. (22-24) Be bold, because **you have come to Mount Zion**.

But you have come to Mount Zion and to the city of the living God, the heavenly Jerusalem, to an innumerable company of angels, to the general assembly and church of the firstborn *who are* registered in heaven, to God the Judge of all, to the spirits of just men made perfect, to Jesus the Mediator of the new covenant, and to the blood of sprinkling that speaks better things than *that of* Abel.

a. **But you have come to Mount Zion**: We are in a different place. Our relationship with God is not modeled after Israel's experience on Mount Sinai. We come to God's other mountain: Zion, the name of the hill upon which Jerusalem sits. The law came to Sinai; the cross was on Zion.

b. **The city of the living God**: There was no city at Mount Sinai; it was out in the desolate desert.

c. **The heavenly Jerusalem**: Sinai was associated with Egypt; Zion is associated with heaven.

d. **To an innumerable company of angels**: A few angels delivered the law to Moses on Mount Sinai; yet Mount Zion has **an innumerable company of angels**.

e. **To the general assembly and church of the firstborn who are registered in heaven**: What God gave at Mount Sinai was mainly for Israel; what God gave at Mount Zion is for all and it spans all the redeemed, both the **church** and **the general assembly** of the redeemed, all together.

f. **To God the Judge of all, and to the spirits of just men made perfect**: Mount Zion doesn't do away with God as **Judge of all** - not at all. Rather, the work Jesus did on Mount Zion satisfies the justice of God, bringing forth **the spirits of just men made perfect**.

g. **To Jesus the Mediator of the new covenant**: Mount Sinai was all about an old covenant based on earning and deserving. Mount Zion is based on a **new covenant** with **Jesus the Mediator** based on believing and receiving.

h. **To the blood of sprinkling that speaks of better things than that of Abel**: The **blood of Abel** does not mean the blood he shed in his martyrdom. Rather, it was the blood of the sacrifice he made - the first recorded sacrifice from man to God in the Bible. The blood of Jesus **speaks better things** than the blood of animal sacrifice, the blood of Abel.

i. Yet it is true that the blood of Jesus the Messiah **speaks better things than that of** the blood of Abel the martyr. The blood of Abel cried, *justice must be satisfied, bring vengeance*. The blood of Jesus cried, *justice has been satisfied, bring mercy*.

i. **But you have come to Mount Zion**: The lesson is plain. We shouldn't come to Mount Zion as if we were coming to Mount Sinai. So put away your hesitation, be encouraged and get bold in coming to God.

i. Consider the contrasts between Mount Sinai and Mount Zion.

- Mount Sinai was marked by fear and terror - Mount Zion is a place of love and forgiveness.

- Mount Sinai is in the desert - Mount Zion is the city of the Living God.

- Mount Sinai spoke of earthly things - Mount Zion speaks of heavenly things.

- At Mount Sinai, only Moses was allowed to draw near to God - at Mount Zion, an **innumerable company**, a **general assembly** is invited to draw near.

- Mount Sinai was characterized by guilty men in fear - Mount Zion features **just men made perfect**.

- At Mount Sinai, Moses was the mediator - at Mount Zion, Jesus is the mediator.

- Mount Sinai brought an Old Covenant, which was ratified by the blood of animals - Mount Zion brought a New Covenant, which is ratified by the blood of God's precious Son.

- Mount Sinai was all about exclusion, keeping people away from the mountain - Mount Zion is all about invitation.

- Mount Sinai is all about Law - Mount Zion is all about grace.

ii. Of course, the idea of the superiority of the New Covenant is also repeated. It shows that these Jewish Christians should not even consider going back and preferring the religion of Mount Sinai to the relationship of Mount Zion.

5. (25-26) Watch out; great privilege has a great warning and danger within it.

See that you do not refuse Him who speaks. For if they did not escape who refused Him who spoke on earth, much more *shall we not escape* if we turn away from Him who *speaks* from heaven, whose voice then shook the earth; but now He has promised, saying, "Yet once more I shake not only the earth, but also heaven."

a. **See that you do not refuse Him who speaks**: As described in the previous verses, God holds the goodness and glory of Mount Zion before us - the perfect and finished work of Jesus and the New Covenant through Him. If we choose to **refuse** this from God, we can't ignore the consequences.

b. **They did not escape**: There were consequences for rebelling at Mount Sinai. There are and should be even greater consequences for resisting God's greater work at Mount Zion.

c. **Whose voice then shook the earth... Yet once more I shake not only the earth, but also heaven**: At Mount Sinai God shook the earth with His voice. *The New Covenant shakes things up even more* (**Yet once more I shake not only the earth, but also heaven**).

i. It's easy - and dangerous - to think that God was severe and mean in the Old Testament and somehow became nice in the New Testament. This is so simplistic that it is deceiving - there is more mercy in the Old Testament than many imagine, and there is more judgment in the New Testament than many imagine.

ii. When everything is shaken the only question is, *where are you standing? Is it safe and secure?*

6. (27) Why God shakes the existing order.

Now this, "Yet once more," indicates the removal of those things that are being shaken, as of things that are made, that the things which cannot be shaken may remain.

a. **Indicates the removal of those things that are being shaken**: God promises to shake things again to take away (**the removal**) reliance on the material - as in material things, materialism.

b. **That the things which cannot be shaken may remain**: God shakes things to *test* them, and then to *take away* the things that can't take the test.

7. (28-29) The unshakable kingdom.

Therefore, since we are receiving a kingdom which cannot be shaken, let us have grace, by which we may serve God acceptably with reverence and godly fear. For our God *is* a consuming fire.

a. **Since we are receiving a kingdom which cannot be shaken**: In contrast to the instability of the world around us, the **kingdom** of Jesus **cannot be shaken**, and **we are receiving** this kingdom.

i. *This is our stability in an unstable world.* We don't yet full have this kingdom; it is yet to come. Yet **we are receiving it**. Griffith Thomas noted that the ancient grammar and phrasing indicates "We are constantly and perpetually (Greek) receiving a Kingdom that is incapable of being shaken."

ii. How we have already received the kingdom

- We have received it in *promise*; a promise from a trustworthy man is just as sure as having the thing itself.

- We have it in *principle*, and we see the principles of God's kingdom at work in the world.

- We have received it in *power*, and see the life-changing and miraculous power of God at work in the world today.

- We have received *some of the provision and protection* of the kingdom, because our King provides for and protects us.

- We have in received it in community, for our congregational gatherings are kingdom communities.

b. **Let us have grace**: The kingdom itself will never be shaken. So we must seize God's unmerited approval in Jesus, helping us to **serve God acceptably**.

i. "Glory be to God, our kingdom cannot be moved! Not even dynamite can touch our dominion: no power in the world, and no power in hell, can shake the kingdom which the Lord has given to his saints. With Jesus as our monarch we fear no revolution and no anarchy: for the Lord hath established this kingdom upon a rock, and it cannot be moved or removed." (Spurgeon)

ii. **We may serve God acceptably**: These words explain just how this may be done.

- Our acceptable service begins with our being receivers (**since we are receiving a kingdom**).

- Our acceptable service is offered by the work of God's grace in us (**let us have grace**).

- Our acceptable service is marked by reverence (**with reverence**).

- Our acceptable service is marked by the spirit of happy reverence (**with godly fear**).

- Our acceptable service is marked by a profound sense of the divine holiness (**for our God is a consuming fire**).

iii. Some wrongly argue that "too much" grace gives license and breeds disrespect towards God. Actually, grace gives us **reverence and godly fear**. Perhaps those who think grace gives them license to sin aren't walking in grace at all.

c. **Our God is a consuming fire**: Since God is in fact a **consuming fire**, we do best to come to Him on *His* terms. These are the terms of unmerited approval in Jesus. He will consume all that is outside of that sphere.

i. Elijah knew that God was a consuming fire; He consumed the sacrifice at the altar on Mount Carmel. Solomon knew that God was a consuming fire; He consumed the sacrifice at the altar at the dedication of the temple.

ii. The truth that **God is a consuming fire** is a *comfort* to the believer. They realize that the Father poured out His **consuming fire** of judgment on the Son in our place. When He did, it completely *consumed* the guilt of sin in all who believe. The penalty of sin was *consumed* in Jesus at the cross.

Hebrews 13 - Living A Positive Christian Life

A. Instructions for body life.

1. (1-3) General love among believers: express brotherly love.

Let brotherly love continue. Do not forget to entertain strangers, for by so *doing* some have unwittingly entertained angels. Remember the prisoners as if chained with them—those who are mistreated—since you yourselves are in the body also.

a. **Let brotherly love continue**: The writer to the Hebrews used the ancient Greek word *philadelphia* here. He *assumed* there was **brotherly love** among Christians, and simply asked that it would **continue** among them.

i. In the ancient Greek language of the New Testament, there were four words at hand that we might translate *love*.

- *Eros* was one word for love. It described, as we might guess from the word itself, *erotic* love, referring to sexual love.

- *Storge* was a second word for love. It referred to family love, the kind of love there is between a parent and child or between family members in general.

- *Agape* was another word for love. It is the most powerful word for *love* in the New Testament, and was often used to describe God's love towards us. It is a love that loves without changing. It is a self-giving love that gives without demanding or expecting re-payment. It is love so great that it can be given to the unlovable or unappealing. It is love that loves even when it is rejected. *Agape* love gives and loves because it wants to; it does not demand or expect repayment from the love given - it gives because it loves, it does not love in order to receive. *Agape* love isn't about *feelings*; it is about *decisions*.

152

ii. But the word for **love** used in Hebrews 13:1 is *philadelphia*, coming from the root *philia*. This ancient Greek word spoke of brotherly friendship and affection. It is the love of deep friendship and partnership. There should always be plenty of this kind of love among Christians, and it should **continue**.

b. **Do not forget to entertain strangers**: This is a simple and practical way that **brotherly love** should **continue** among believers. Hospitality is an important virtue and often it is commanded of Christians and leaders (Romans 12:10-13, 1 Timothy 3:2, Titus 1:7-8, 1 Peter 4:9). In the ancient world, where inns did exist, were notorious for immorality. It was important for traveling Christians to find open homes from other Christians.

i. Because of this command of hospitality, Christians had to watch out for people just masquerading as Christians so they could leech off the generosity of God's people. As time went on, Christian leaders taught their people how to recognize these deceivers.

ii. The Didache was an early church "ministry manual," written perhaps somewhere between A.D. 90 and 110. It had this to say about how to tell if a false prophet abused the hospitality of those in the church:

Let every apostle that comes to you be received as the Lord. But he shall not remain except one day; but if there be need, also the next; but if he remains three days, he is a false prophet. And when the apostle goes away, let him take nothing but bread... but if he asks for money, he is a false prophet. And every prophet that speaks in the Spirit you shall neither try nor judge; for every sin shall be forgiven, but this one sin shall not be forgiven. But not everyone that speaks in the Spirit is a prophet; but only if he holds the ways of the Lord. Therefore from their ways shall the false prophet and the true prophet be known. (From *The Ante-Nicean Fathers*, Volume 7, page 380)

c. **Strangers**: The point was that they were to do this for other Christians who are **strangers** to us. If you invite your best friends over for lunch, that is wonderful - but it doesn't fulfill this command. A wonderful way to fulfill this command is to meet and befriend **strangers** at church and to **entertain** them with hospitality.

i. The ancient Greek word for *hospitality* (used in passages like Romans 12:13) is literally translated, "love for strangers." **Brotherly love** means love for all our brothers and sisters in Jesus, not just those who are currently our friends.

d. **For by so doing some have unwittingly entertained angels**: When we are hospitable to others, we really welcome Jesus (Matthew 25:35), and perhaps angels. Abraham (Genesis 18:1-22) and Lot (Genesis 19:1-3) are examples of those who **unwittingly entertained angels**.

e. **Remember the prisoners as if chained with them**: **Prisoners** here probably has first reference to those imprisoned for the sake of the Gospel. But it can also be extended to all who are in prison. We must serve them with a sympathetic heart (**as if chained with them**). This is just another way to **let brotherly love continue**.

i. We do this by doing what we call prison ministry, bringing the truth and love and hope of Jesus to those imprisoned.

ii. We do this by remembering those who are imprisoned for the sake of the gospel, such as the many now imprisoned in the Middle East.

2. (4) Honor marital love.

Marriage *is* honorable among all, and the bed undefiled; but fornicators and adulterers God will judge.

a. **Marriage is honorable among all**: The Bible holds high the ideal of married life and the institution of family.

i. This is difficult to speak about today, because many who aren't married feel put off by an emphasis on marriage and family in the church.

ii. This is difficult to speak about today, because this (**marriage is honorable among all**) is becoming less and less true in the society as a whole.

* Marriage is dishonored by divorce, justified or not.
* Marriage is dishonored by living together outside of marriage.
* Marriage is dishonored by adultery.
* Marriage is dishonored by neglect.
* Marriage is dishonored by re-definition.

b. **Marriage is honorable among all, and the bed undefiled**: This is another place where the Bible celebrates sex as an expression of married love. This is the consistent teaching of the Bible, in such places as The Song of Solomon.

i. The Bible speaks powerfully about the purpose of sex.

* Not just for reproduction, though that is an aspect.
* Not just for pleasure, though that is an aspect.

- The main purpose is to bond together a one-flesh relationship. This is what gives sex meaning, beyond a pleasurable experience; this is what God offers in sexual expression according to His will, what the world can't offer or match.

ii. With this perspective, we see why God commands what He does in regard to sex and why God says, **and the bed undefiled**. It also explains why the enemy of our souls wants to do everything he can to en̲courage sex *outside* of the marriage **bed** and he wants to do everything he can to di̲scourage sex *inside* the marriage **bed**. Christians must recognize this strategy and not give it a foothold.

iii. Though God allows great freedom in the variety of sexual expression in marriage, all must be done with a concern for the needs of their spouse and in love (1 Corinthians 7:2-5 and Ephesians 5:21-33).

c. **But fornicators and adulterers God will judge**: As the Bible celebrates sexual expression in marriage, it also condemns sex outside of the marriage commitment. God does this because *fornication* and *adultery* work against God's greatest purpose for sex (though they may fulfill the *pleasure* purpose).

- In this context, **fornicators** refers to those who have sex without the commitment of marriage.

- In this context, **adulterers** refers to those who are not faithful to their marriage vows and have sex outside of their marriage vows.

- i. "Fornication and adultery are not synonymous in the New Testament: adultery implies unfaithfulness by either party to the marriage vow, while the word translated 'fornication' covers a wide range of sexual irregularities." (Bruce)

3. (5-6) Learn contentment over covetousness.

Let your **conduct** *be* **without covetousness;** *be* **content with such things as you have. For He Himself has said, "I will never leave you nor forsake you." So we may boldly say:**

"The Lord *is* my helper;
I will not fear.
What can man do to me?"

a. **Let your conduct be without covetousness; be content**: Covetousness is the opposite of *contentment*. Often **covetousness** and greed are excused or even admired in today's culture, and are simply called *ambition*.

b. **Be content with such things as you have**: Contentment has much more to do with what you *are* on the inside rather than what you *have*. The Apostle Paul had the right idea in Philippians 4:11-13: *Not that I speak in* *regard to need, for I have learned in whatever state I am, to be content: I know how to be abased, and I know how to abound. Everywhere and in all things I have learned both to be full and to be hungry, both to abound and to suffer need. I can do all things through Christ who strengthens me.*

i. Someone asked millionaire Bernard Baruch, "How much money does it take for a rich man to be satisfied?" Baruch answered, "Just a million more than he has."

c. **I will never leave you nor forsake you**: This promise from God (from Deuteronomy 31:6) is the foundation for contentment. We can't count on material things, but we can depend on God and His promise.

i. "You that are familiar with the Greek text know that there are five negatives here. We cannot manage five negatives in English, but the Greeks find them not too large a handful. Here the negatives have a fivefold force. It is as though it said, 'I will not, not leave thee; I will never, no never, forsake thee.'" (Spurgeon)

ii. "Here it is - 'For he hath said, I will never leave thee, nor forsake thee.' This is the reason why we must not be covetous. There is no room to be covetous, no excuse for being covetous, for God hath said, 'I will never leave thee, nor forsake thee.' We ought to be content. If we are not content, we are acting insanely, seeing the Lord has said, 'I will never leave thee, nor forsake thee.'" (Spurgeon)

iii. "I cannot under the influence of this grand text find room for doubt or fear. I cannot stand here and be miserable to-night. I am not going to attempt such a thing; but I cannot be despondent with such a text as this, 'I will never leave thee, nor forsake thee.' I defy the devil himself to mention circumstances under which I ought to be miserable if this text is true. Child of God, nothing ought to make you unhappy when you can realize this precious text." (Spurgeon)

d. **So we may boldly say: "The LORD is my helper; I will not fear. What can man do to me?"** This quotation from Psalm 118:6 points to the truth that real contentment comes only when we trust in God to meet our needs and to be our security. Strangely we are often more likely to put security and find contentment in *things* that are far less reliable and secure than God Himself is.

4. (7) Follow your leaders.

Remember those who rule over you, who have spoken the word of God to you, whose faith follow, considering the outcome of *their* conduct.

a. **Remember those who rule over you**: We are told to recognize and follow godly leadership in the body of Christ, leadership shown to be legitimate by faithfulness to the **word of God** and by godly **conduct**.

i. Paul advised Timothy along the same lines: *Take heed to yourself and to the doctrine. Continue in them, for in doing this you will save both yourself and those who hear you.* (1 Timothy 4:16)

b. **Whose faith follow**: Such leaders should be recognized (**remember those**) and followed. Just as much as a church needs godly leaders, it also needs godly *followers*.

c. **Considering the outcome of their conduct**: Leaders don't need to be perfect, but they should be able to show with their life that the power of Jesus is real as it impacts and transforms the individual life. That demonstrates a faith that can actually be followed.

B. Instructions in worship.

1. (8) The enduring principle: the unchanging nature of Jesus.

Jesus Christ *is* the same yesterday, today, and forever.

a. **Jesus Christ is the same**: The unchanging nature (which theologians call *immutability*) of Jesus Christ could be inferred from His deity, even if it were not explicitly stated. God doesn't change over the ages, so neither does Jesus, who is God.

b. **Yesterday, today, and forever**: His unchanging nature provides a measure for all Christian conduct, particularly in the word and in worship. We should not expect something completely "new" as if it were from a "new Jesus." The nature of Jesus as it is revealed in the Bible is the same nature of Jesus that should be seen in the church today.

2. (9-14) Following the rejected Jesus.

Do not be carried about with various and strange doctrines. For *it is* good that the heart be established by grace, not with foods which have not profited those who have been occupied with them. We have an altar from which those who serve the tabernacle have no right to eat. For the bodies of those animals, whose blood is brought into the sanctuary by the high priest for sin, are burned outside the camp. Therefore Jesus also, that He might sanctify the people with His own blood, suffered outside the gate. Therefore let us go forth to Him, outside the camp, bearing His reproach. For here we have no continuing city, but we seek the one to come.

a. **Do not be carried about with various and strange doctrines**: There is never a shortage of **various and strange doctrines** in the church. The ones specifically in mind here seem to deal with a return to Mosaic ceremonies and laws that were fulfilled in Jesus.

b. **For it is good that the heart be established by grace**: Our hearts will only be **established by grace**. We are **established** by an understanding and appropriation of God's undeserved approval of us, and not by an assumed approval gained through keeping a list of rules (**not with foods which have not profited those who have been occupied with them**).

c. **We have an altar from which those who serve the tabernacle have no right to eat**: Their friends and relatives remaining in traditional Judaism labeled these Jewish Christians *illegitimate* because they did not continue the Levitical system. But the writer to the Hebrews insisted that **we have an altar**, and it is an altar that those who cling to the Levitical system have no **right** to.

   i. Essentially, our **altar** is the cross - the centerpiece of the Christian gospel and understanding (1 Corinthians 1:18-24 and 1 Corinthians 2:1-5).

d. **Jesus... suffered outside the gate. Therefore let us go forth to Him, outside the camp, bearing His reproach**: If our Savior was rejected and His sacrifice (performed at the cross, our **altar**) was considered illegitimate then we expect nothing better. Identifying with Jesus often means **bearing His reproach**, the very thing many are unwilling to do.

   i. **Outside the camp**: The **camp** refers to institutional Judaism, which rejected Jesus and Christianity. Though these Christians from Jewish backgrounds were raised to consider everything **outside the camp** as unclean and evil, now they had follow Jesus **outside** traditional, institutional Judaism of that time.

   ii. "It means, first, let us have fellowship with him. He was despised; he had no credit for charity; he was mocked in the streets; lie was hissed at; he was hounded from among society. If I take a smooth part, I can have no fellowship with him: fellowship requires a like experience." (Spurgeon)

   iii. "A sorry life your Master had, you see. All the filth in earth's kennels was thrown at him by sacrilegious hands. No epithet was thought coarse enough; no terms hard enough; he was the song of the drunkard, and they that sat in the gate spoke against him. This was the reproach of Christ; and we are not to marvel if we bear as much. 'Well,' says one, 'I will not be a Christian if I am to bear that.' Skulk back, then, you coward, to your own damnation; but oh! Men that love God, and who seek after the eternal reward, I pray you do not shrink from this cross. You must bear it." (Spurgeon)

iv. "If you can dwell with the wicked, if you can live as they live, and be 'hail-fellow well met' with the ungodly, if their practices are your practices, if their pleasures are your pleasures, then their god is your god, and you are one of them. There is no being a Christian without being shut out of the world's camp." (Spurgeon)

e. **For here we have no continuing city, but we seek the one to come**: The difficult job of **bearing His reproach** is easier when we remember that the city or society we are cast out from is only temporary. We **seek** and belong to the permanent city yet to come.

i. In **bearing His reproach** we face great difficulty and suffering. The good news is that for those who bear **His reproach**, this world is the *worst* they will ever have it. For cowards who turn their back on Jesus, this life is the absolute *best* they will ever have it.

3. (15-16) Our sacrifice.

Therefore by Him let us continually offer the sacrifice of praise to God, that is, the fruit of *our* lips, giving thanks to His name. But do not forget to do good and to share, for with such sacrifices God is well pleased.

a. **Therefore by Him let us continually offer the sacrifice of praise to God**: Because we do have an *altar* (the cross) and we do have a High Priest (Jesus), we should always offer sacrifices. Yet they are not the bloody sacrifices of the old covenant but the **sacrifice of praise**, the **fruit of our lips**.

i. The writer to the Hebrews explains several essentials for proper praise.

- Praise that pleases God is offered **by Him**, that is **by** Jesus Christ, on the ground of His righteousness and pleasing God.

- Praise that pleases God is offered **continually**, so that we are always praising Him.

- Praise that pleases God is a **sacrifice of praise**, in that it may be costly or inconvenient.

- Praise that pleases God is **the fruit of our lips**, more than just thoughts directed towards God. It is spoken out unto the Lord, either is prose or in song. "What proceeds from the lips is regarded as *fruit*, which reveals the character of its source, as the fruit of a tree reveals the nature of the tree." (Guthrie)

ii. "Loving hearts must speak. What would you think of a husband who never felt any impulse to tell his wife that she was dear to him; or a mother who never found it needful to unpack her heart of its tenderness, even in perhaps the inarticulate croonings over the little child that she pressed to her heart? It seems to me that a dumb Christian, a man who is thankful for Christ's sacrifice and never feels the need to say so, is as great an anomaly as either of these I have described." (Maclaren)

iii. "So, then, we are *to utter* the praises of God, and it is not sufficient *to feel* adoring emotions." (Spurgeon)

b. **But do not forget to do good and to share, for with such sacrifices God is well pleased**: Praise is not the only sacrifice that pleases God. We also please God with sacrifice when we **do good** and **share**. Praise and worship are important, but the Christian's obligation does not end there.

4. (17) Follow your leaders.

Obey those who rule over you, and be submissive, for they watch out for your souls, as those who must give account. Let them do so with joy and not with grief, for that would be unprofitable for you.

a. **Obey those who rule over you, and be submissive**: We are to **be submissive** to the leaders God gives us (assuming they have the character mentioned in Hebrews 13:7). We are simply told to **obey those who rule** over us. When speaking on the authority of God's Word, leaders *do* have a right to tell us how to live and walk after God.

i. Sadly, some take the idea of submission to leaders in the church much too far. The "Shepherding Movement" was a clear example of this kind of abuse (which many seem to welcome, wanting someone else to be responsible for their lives). "A teacher should teach us to submit to God, not to himself." (Chuck Smith)

b. **As those who must give account**: We **obey** and **submit** to our leaders because God put them in a place of responsibility and accountability over us. Of course, this does not relieve individual responsibility but it puts an *additional* accountability and responsibility upon leaders.

c. **Let them do so with joy and not with grief, for that would be unprofitable for you**: Cooperative conduct is not only a joy to leaders, but it is profitable for the whole body. It is for *our own sake* that we should **obey** and **submit** to God-appointed leaders.

C. Concluding remarks.

1. (18-19) A request for prayer.

Pray for us; for we are confident that we have a good conscience, in all things desiring to live honorably. But I especially urge *you* to do this, that I may be restored to you the sooner.

a. **Pray for us**: The writer to the Hebrews considered it important that others pray for him. We all need and should welcome the prayers of others.

i. In the grammar of the ancient Greek language, **pray** is in the *present imperative* verb tense. It indicates continuous activity and implies that they were already praying for him.

b. **That I may be restored to you the sooner**: Obstacles prevented the writer from being reunited with his readers. He knew that prayer could remove those obstacles.

i. **I especially urge you to do this**: As far as the writer to the Hebrews was concerned their prayers determined *if* and *when* he is reunited with them. This shows how seriously he regarded their prayers for him.

2. (20-21) A blessing is pronounced.

Now may the God of peace who brought up our Lord Jesus from the dead, that great Shepherd of the sheep, through the blood of the everlasting covenant, make you complete in every good work to do His will, working in you what is well pleasing in His sight, through Jesus Christ, to whom *be* glory forever and ever. Amen.

a. **Now may the God of peace**: This is a blessing in the style of the priestly blessing of Numbers 6:22-27: *The LORD bless you and keep you; the LORD make His face shine upon you, and be gracious to you; the LORD lift up His countenance upon you, and give you peace.*

i. After asking his readers to pray for him, the writer to the Hebrews prays for his readers. "The apostle had exhorted the Hebrew believers to pray for him in the words, 'Pray for us;' and then, as if to show that he did not ask of them what he was not himself. Willing to give, he utters this most wonderful prayer for them. He may confidently say to his congregation, 'Pray for me' who does unfeignedly from his soul pray for them." (Spurgeon)

b. **Now may the God of peace**: In this blessing God is first recognized in His attributes: **peace**, power (**brought up our Lord Jesus from the dead**), loving care (**that great Shepherd**), and ever giving love (**the blood of the everlasting covenant**).

i. Some take the idea of **the everlasting covenant** to express the **covenant** that existed before the foundation of the world between the Persons of the Godhead, working together for the salvation of man.

Other passages which may speak to this **everlasting covenant** are Revelation 13:8, Ephesians 1:4, and 2 Timothy 1:9.

ii. Some however simply take **the everlasting covenant** as another name for the New Covenant.

c. **Make you complete in every good work**: This expresses the desire for blessing, wanting God's **working in you**, and all **through Jesus Christ**.

3. (22-25) Conclusion to the letter to the Hebrews.

And I appeal to you, brethren, bear with the word of exhortation, for I have written to you in few words. Know that *our* brother Timothy has been set free, with whom I shall see you if he comes shortly. Greet all those who rule over you, and all the saints. Those from Italy greet you. Grace *be* with you all. Amen.

a. **Bear with the word of exhortation, for I have written to you in few words**: The writer to the Hebrews reminds us of his purpose. His desire was to write a **word of exhortation** to encourage discouraged Christians, both then and now.

i. In Acts 13:15 the phrase **word of exhortation** refers to a sermon. Perhaps the writer to the Hebrews means in Hebrews 13:22 that he gives his readers a written sermon.

b. **Know that our brother Timothy has been set free, with whom I shall see you if he comes shortly**: These final words give us a few tantalizing hints of the writer's identity. But these words only tell us that the writer knew **Timothy** and that he planned to visit his readers soon. It also tells us that his readers were based in Italy (**Those from Italy greet you**), probably in the city of Rome.

c. **Grace be with you all**: This is a fitting end for a book that documents the passing of the Old Covenant and the institution of the New Covenant. **Grace be with you all** indeed, under what God has given through the superior Savior, Jesus Christ! **Amen!**

Bibliography - Hebrews

Alford, Henry *The New Testament for English Readers, Volume II, Part II* (London: Rivingtons, 1869)

Barclay, William *The Letter to the Hebrews* (Philadelphia: Westminster Press, 1975)

Barnes, Albert *Barnes on the New Testament: Hebrews* (Grand Rapids, Michigan: Baker Book House, 1975)

Brown, John *The Epistle to the Hebrews* (Edinburgh, Great Britain: The Banner of Truth Trust, 1983 reprint of 1862 edition)

Bruce, A.B. *The Epistle to the Hebrews* (Minneapolis, Minnesota: Klock & Klock Christian Publishers, 1980 reprint of 1899 edition)

Bruce, F.F. *The Epistle to the Hebrews* (Grand Rapids, Michigan: Eerdmans Publishing Company, 1964)

Calvin, John *Hebrews and I and II Peter*, translated by W.B. Johnston (Grand Rapids, Michigan: Eerdmans, 1963)

Clarke, Adam *The New Testament with A Commentary and Critical Notes, Volume II* (New York: Eaton & Mains, 1831)

Dods, Marcus "The Epistle to the Hebrews" *The Expositor's Greek Testament, Volume IV* (London, Hodder and Stoughton Limited: ?)

Guthrie, Donald *Hebrews* (Grand Rapids, Michigan: Eerdmans Publishing Company, 1983)

Lenski, R.C.H. *The Interpretation of The Epistle to the Hebrews and The Epistle of James* (Minneapolis, Minnesota: Augsburg Publishing House, 1966)

Lightfoot, J.B. *St. Paul's Epistles to the Colossians and to Philemon* (Lynn, Massachusetts: Hendrickson Publishers, 1982)

Maclaren, Alexander *Expostions of Holy Scripture, Volume Fifteen* and *Expositions of Holy Scripture, Volume Sixteen* (Grand Rapids, Michigan: Baker, 1984)

Meyer, F.B. *The Way Into the Holiest: Expositions of the Epistle to the Hebrews* (Fort Washington, Pennsylvania: Christian Literature Crusade, 1982)

Morgan, G. Campbell *An Exposition of the Whole Bible* (Old Tappan, New Jersey: Revell, 1959)

Morris, Leon "Hebrews" *The Expositor's Bible Commentary Volume 12* (Grand Rapids, Michigan: Zondervan Publishing House, 1981)

Morris, Leon "1 Timothy-James" *Daily Bible Commentary, Romans to Revelation* (Philadelphia, A.J. Holman Company: 1974)

Newell, William R. *Hebrews Verse by Verse* (Chicago: Moody Press, 1947)

Owen, John Hebrews: *The Epistle of Warning* (Grand Rapids, Michigan: Kregel, 1985)

Poole, Matthew *A Commentary on the Holy Bible, Volume III: Matthew-Revelation* (London: Banner of Truth Trust, 1969, first published in 1685)

Robertson, Archibald T. *Word Pictures in the New Testament, Volume V* (Nashville: Broadman Press, 1933)

Smith, Chuck *New Testament Study Guide* (Costa Mesa, California: The Word for Today, 1982)

Spurgeon, Charles Haddon *The New Park Street Pulpit, Volumes 1-6* and *The Metropolitan Tabernacle Pulpit, Volumes 7-63* (Pasadena, Texas: Pilgrim Publications, 1990)

Trapp, John *A Commentary on the Old and New Testaments, Volume Five* (Eureka, California: Tanski Publications, 1997)

Vincent, Marvin R. *Vincent's Word Studies of the New Testament, Volume IV* (McLean, Virginia: MacDonald, ?)

Wiersbe, Warren W. *The Bible Exposition Commentary, Volume 2* (Wheaton, Illinios: Victor Books, 1989)

As the years pass I love the work of studying, learning, and teaching the Bible more than ever. I'm so grateful that God is faithful to meet me in His Word.

Much thanks to the many who helped prepare this commentary. The year this commentary was first published (2004) was a tremendous year of change for our whole family, and my gratitude goes out to my wife Inga-Lill and our children who give so much support in this and all the ministry.

Once again I enjoyed the capable proofreading help of Martina Patrick. Our friendship with the Patricks is both long and deep - and we especially want to thank Martina for all her hard work on this commentary. Martina, you and Tim are special partners in our work.

Thanks to Brian Procedo for the cover design and all the graphics work.

Most especially, thanks to my wife Inga-Lill. She is my loved and valued partner in life and in service to God and His people.

David Guzik

David Guzik's Bible commentary is regularly used and trusted by many thousands who want to know the Bible better. Pastors, teachers, class leaders, and everyday Christians find his commentary helpful for their own understanding and explanation of the Bible. David and his wife Inga-Lill live in Santa Barbara, California.

You can email David at
david@enduringword.com

For more resources by David Guzik,
go to www.enduringword.com

Printed in the USA
CPSIA information can be obtained
at www.ICGtesting.com
JSHW022024231023
50704JS00003B/13